FROM POSTS TO PROFITS

A REALTOR'S PLAYBOOK FOR BUILDING A THRIVING REAL ESTATE BUSINESS THROUGH SOCIAL MEDIA AND BRAND INFLUENCE

RANDI LYNN QUIGLEY

Copyright © 2024 Randi Lynn Quigley

All rights reserved. This publication, or any part thereof, may not be reproduced in any form or by any means, including electronic, photographic, or mechanical, or by any sound recording system or by any device for storage and retrieval of information without the written permission of the copyright owner.

Disclaimer

The content in this book is intended for informational and educational purposes only. The strategies, techniques, and recommendations outlined in this book are based on the author's personal experience, research, and expertise. Results may vary, and the success of implementing these strategies depends on various factors, including individual effort, market conditions, and adherence to legal and professional standards.

Readers are encouraged to consult with legal, financial, and real estate professionals before implementing any advice contained in this book to ensure compliance with applicable laws, regulations, and industry practices. The author and publisher disclaim any liability for any losses or damages resulting from the use of the information in this book.

Social media platforms, algorithms, and trends are subject to change. Readers are advised to stay updated on platform policies and adapt strategies accordingly. This book does not guarantee any specific results, financial outcomes, or business growth.

By using the information in this book, you agree to take full responsibility for your actions and outcomes.

Dedication

This book is dedicated to every real estate professional who dreams of building something extraordinary, even when the odds seem impossible. To those who face challenges head-on and refuse to give up—this is for you.

To my incredible family, thank you for your love, patience, and unwavering support. To my children, Aiden, Chelsea, Jacub, and Faye, you are my greatest inspiration and the reason I strive to be my best every day. To my husband, Steve—thank you for all you do for our family. And to my clients and followers, your trust and belief in me have made this journey so rewarding.

For anyone starting from scratch, know this: no matter your circumstances, with determination, authenticity, and the right strategy, you can create a life and career beyond your wildest dreams.

About the Author

Randi Lynn Quigley's journey is a testament to resilience, determination, and the power of starting over. Beginning her career as a single mom of three—Aiden, Chelsea, and Jacub—Randi faced seemingly insurmountable odds but built her real estate business from the ground up. With hard work, grit, and a deep belief in her vision, she created a nationally recognized brand that has achieved over $200 million in career sales.

Now remarried to her husband, Steve, and raising a beautiful family of four children, including her youngest, Faye, Randi has become a trailblazer in the real estate world. She transformed her challenges into opportunities, mastering the art of authentic connection and using social media to build trust and loyalty with her audience.

In *From Posts to Profits*, Randi shares the strategies and insights that helped her grow a thriving real estate business and an influential personal brand. Her story proves that no matter where you start, with passion and perseverance, you can achieve remarkable success.

Contents

Your Roadmap to Real Estate Success	11
1. Establishing Your Brand Foundation	17
2. Mastering Authentic Engagement	25
3. Identifying and Targeting Your Ideal Audience	35
4. Platform-Specific Strategies for Realtors	41
5. Content Creation and Curation Mastery	47
6. Building and Nurturing a Brand Community	53
7. Building an Irresistible Personal Brand	59
8. Scaling Your Presence for Exponential Growth	65
9. Converting Followers into Clients	71
10. Turning Clients into Advocates	77
11. Mastering Your Local Market	83
12. Sustaining Success Through Adaptability and Growth	89
13. Leveraging Technology to Elevate Your Business	95
14. Building a Team and Expanding Your Reach	101
15. Overcoming Challenges in Real Estate	107
16. The Psychology of Selling	113
17. The Future of Real Estate: Embracing Change and Defining Your Path	119
Bonus Chapter: Coaching with Cardone—Taking Real Estate to the Next Level	125
My Journey	135
A Note to the Reader	141

Your Roadmap to Real Estate Success

When I started my journey in real estate, I didn't know what to expect. Like many new agents, I was filled with excitement, uncertainty, and an overwhelming desire to succeed. I didn't have a perfect plan, a long list of clients, or even a clear understanding of what this career would demand from me. What I did have was vision, determination, and a belief that I could create a life I loved while helping others do the same.

This book isn't just about selling homes or building a business—it's about creating a legacy. It's about showing up every day, ready to learn, adapt, and make a difference. Whether you're just starting out in real estate, looking to take your career to the next level, or simply seeking inspiration, this book is for you.

I'll be honest: real estate isn't for the faint of heart. It's a world of high stakes, emotional decisions, and constant change. But it's also one of the most rewarding, exciting, and impactful industries you can be a part of. Every transaction is a chance to change someone's life—and your own.

The Beginning of My Journey

Let me take you back to where it all started. I grew up in a modest three-bedroom condo, surrounded by lessons of hard work and resilience. My parents worked tirelessly to provide for our family, and their example instilled in me the belief that anything is possible with dedication and effort.

After college, I followed a traditional path into accounting. It was steady, predictable, and secure—but it wasn't fulfilling. I found myself yearning for something more, something that would challenge me, inspire me, and allow me to make a tangible impact. That's when real estate entered my life.

I didn't know much about the industry when I began. I didn't have a network of wealthy clients or years of experience to lean on. What I did have was a deep desire to connect with people and help them achieve their dreams. I immersed myself in learning, soaking up every piece of advice, training, and wisdom I could find.

My first sale wasn't a multimillion-dollar property; it was a modest home for a young couple starting their journey together. I'll never forget their excitement when they walked through the front door for the first time, knowing it was theirs. That moment cemented my love for real estate. This wasn't just about transactions; it was about transformations.

Real Estate as a Life-Changing Career

What makes real estate so special? For me, it's the fact that every day is different. One day, you're helping a family find their forever home. The next, you're negotiating a deal that changes someone's financial future.

This industry isn't just about homes—it's about people. It's about understanding their needs, their dreams, and their fears. It's about building trust, offering guidance, and creating an experience they'll remember forever.

But real estate is also about you—your growth, your resilience, and your ability to rise to every challenge. It's a career that demands hard work, creativity, and courage. And when you embrace those demands, the rewards are limitless.

The Turning Point: Building My Brand

Early in my career, I realized something important: success in real estate isn't just about knowledge or skill. It's about connections. People don't choose agents based on their credentials alone; they choose someone they trust, someone who understands their unique journey.

This realization led me to focus on building my personal brand. I didn't want to be just another agent; I wanted to be the agent people turned to when they needed someone who cared. I started sharing my story on social media, opening up about my life, my values, and my approach to real estate.

At first, it felt risky. Would people respond to this level of authenticity? Would they see me as a professional? But as I shared more, I realized that people weren't looking for perfection—they were looking for connection. They wanted someone who was real, relatable, and approachable.

This shift wasn't just good for my business; it was good for me. It allowed me to embrace who I truly am and use my unique strengths to serve others. And that's what I want for you, too: a career that feels authentic, fulfilling, and aligned with your values.

Why I Wrote This Book

Over the years, I've been asked countless times, "What's your secret to success?" The truth is there's no single answer. Success is a combination of strategy, mindset, and perseverance. It's about taking risks, learning from failures, and celebrating wins.

I wrote this book because I want to share everything I've learned along the way. I want to show you that no matter where you're starting from, you have the power to build a thriving real estate career—and a life you love.

This book isn't just a guide; it's a conversation. It is a chance for me to share my story, my lessons, and my passion for this industry. It's also an invitation for you to reflect on your own journey and take bold steps toward your goals.

What You'll Learn

This book is packed with actionable advice, real-life stories, and practical strategies for every stage of your career. Here's a glimpse of what's ahead:

1. **Building Your Personal Brand:** How to stand out in a crowded market by being unapologetically yourself.
2. **Mastering Client Relationships:** The art of building trust, understanding psychology, and creating long-term connections.
3. **Embracing Technology:** Leveraging tools like virtual tours, social media, and AI to stay ahead of the curve.
4. **Navigating Challenges:** How to turn setbacks into opportunities and thrive in an ever-changing industry.
5. **Scaling Your Business:** Strategies for building a team, expanding your reach, and creating a legacy.

This book is about more than just tactics—it's about transformation. It's about becoming the best version of yourself, both personally and professionally.

Your "Why"

Before we dive into the chapters, I want to ask you a question: What's your why?

Why are you pursuing this career? Why do you want to grow, succeed, and make an impact? Your why is your compass—it's what will keep you focused and motivated, even on the hardest days.

For me, my why has always been about creating a life that reflects my passions and priorities. It's about helping others achieve their dreams while building a future for my family that I'm proud of. Every decision I make is guided by that purpose, and it's what keeps me going.

A Final Thought

As you turn the pages of this book, I want you to know that everything you need to succeed is already within you. You have the ability to adapt, grow, and thrive in this industry. You have the power to create a career—and a life—that lights you up.

This book is your roadmap, your inspiration, and your reminder that the possibilities are endless. So, take a deep breath, trust yourself, and let's get started.

ONE

Establishing Your Brand Foundation

When I first stepped into real estate, I knew one thing for certain: I had to stand out. The problem? I was walking into an industry filled with seasoned pros who seemed to have everything—years of experience, deep connections, and well-oiled systems. To say it was intimidating would be an understatement. I could have let that discourage me, but instead, I decided to lean into what I *did* have: my story, my vision, and my ability to connect with people authentically. And, as it turns out, those were the most powerful tools I could have ever used to build my brand.

Your brand is so much more than a shiny logo or a catchy tagline. It's the foundation of who you are, what you stand for, and how you show up in the world. It's the core of everything you do in your business. Whether you're a brand-new agent trying to find your footing or a seasoned professional looking to elevate your game, your brand is the foundation that allows you to grow, influence, and scale.

I didn't have it all figured out when I started—far from it. But I knew that if I could tap into what made me unique and show up consistently, I'd create a brand that resonated with clients and stood the test of time.

Finding My Unique Value Proposition

Every brand begins with clarity. In real estate, you're not just selling homes—you're selling trust, expertise, and the promise of results. The first step to building a strong foundation is defining what sets you apart. What makes you different? Why should a client choose you over the agent down the street?

When I started asking myself these questions, I realized that I couldn't compete with years of experience or a portfolio packed with luxury listings. What I could offer was *me*. I was a mom, a community member, and someone who genuinely cared about helping people find their dream homes. I knew how to listen, how to connect, and how to make my clients feel seen. That authenticity became my competitive edge.

I'll never forget one of my first clients, a young couple buying their first home. They didn't choose me because of a slick marketing pitch or fancy accolades—they chose me because I took the time to understand what they wanted, answered their questions with patience, and made them feel confident in their decisions. That experience solidified my belief that people choose people, not resumes.

If you're building your brand, start here: What makes you unique? It could be your deep knowledge of a niche market, your knack for creative problem-solving, or your ability to make the buying or selling process feel effortless. Whatever it is, own it. Your Unique Value Proposition (UVP) is the cornerstone of your brand.

The Power of Storytelling

People don't just buy homes—they buy into you. Your story is one of the most powerful tools you have to connect with your audience on a human level. When I first started sharing my story, I wasn't sure how it would resonate. Would clients care about the challenges I'd faced? Would they find my journey relatable? But the more I leaned into vulnerability, the more I realized how much my story mattered.

I often share how I started from scratch after my divorce, balancing raising kids with building a real estate career. I talked about the late nights, the self-doubt, and the moments I wasn't sure if I could keep going. But I also share how those experiences shaped me—how they taught me resilience, grit, and the value of showing up every day, even when it's hard. That story isn't just about me; it's about my ability to navigate challenges, adapt, and deliver results for my clients.

Storytelling is about more than facts—it's about connection. It's about showing your audience who you are, what you've been through, and how you can help them. When you share your story, you're not just building a brand—you're building trust.

I encourage you to take some time to reflect on your journey. What brought you to real estate? What challenges have you overcome? What values drive you every day? Those pieces of your story are what make you unique, and they're what will draw people to you.

Your Voice is Your Power

Once you've defined your story, it's time to think about how you communicate it. Your brand voice is how you "speak" to your audience—it's the personality that comes through in your marketing, your conversations, and even your social media posts. It's what makes people feel like they know you before they've even met you, and it's a key ingredient in building trust and connection.

When I started developing my brand voice, I knew I wanted it to feel warm, relatable, and approachable. I didn't want to come across as a salesperson spouting industry jargon and memorized pitches. I wanted my audience to feel like they were talking to a trusted friend who happened to be an expert in real estate. This authenticity has been a game-changer for me. It's what helps my message stand out in a sea of sameness and creates a genuine bond with clients before we even speak.

But finding my voice didn't happen overnight. It took trial and error, moments of self-doubt, and a lot of introspection. I remember one of my first social media posts—it was overly polished and felt more like a corporate advertisement than a reflection of who I was. The response? Crickets. It wasn't until I let go of trying to sound "professional" and started writing from the heart that things began to click. I shared a story about juggling work and motherhood, and the response was overwhelming. People resonated with realness, and that's when I realized that my voice wasn't something I had to create—it was something I already had.

Finding your voice is about staying true to who you are. Are you analytical and data-driven? Bold and confident? Friendly and conversational? Whatever your natural style is, embrace it fully. Your voice is the bridge between you and your audience, and the more authentic it is, the stronger that connection will be. Consistency is key—your audience should feel like they know you no matter where they encounter your brand. Whether it's an Instagram post, an email, or a face-to-face meeting, your voice should feel like a reflection of the real you.

The Visual Side of Branding

Your brand isn't just what you say—it's how you present yourself. In today's world, where first impressions often happen online, your visuals matter more than ever. Your logo, colors, and marketing materials are your silent ambassadors, speaking for you before you've had the chance to introduce yourself. They should align seamlessly with your story and values, creating a cohesive identity that clients can instantly recognize and trust.

When I started out, I'll admit, I didn't have a polished visual brand. My marketing materials were a mix of generic templates and last-minute designs, and my social media posts didn't have any consistent look or feel. But as my business grew, I began to see the importance of creating a cohesive visual identity that truly reflected who I was. I invested in professional headshots that captured my personality, worked with a designer to create a sleek logo, and developed a social media aesthetic that felt like an extension of me—modern, approachable, and a little bit bold.

These visual elements weren't just about looking good—they were about building trust and recognition. When a potential client sees your brand consistently across platforms, it sends a powerful message: you're professional, dependable, and intentional about your work. It also helps them remember you. In a crowded industry, visual consistency is what keeps you top-of-mind.

Think of your visuals as your introduction. Before a client reads your bio or hears your pitch, they'll see your branding. What story does it tell? Does it reflect your values, your personality, and the experience you provide? Investing in high-quality visuals is an investment in your reputation. It's not about being flashy—it's about being intentional.

The Commitment to Consistency

Here's the hard truth: building a brand isn't a one-time effort. It's not something you do once; check off your to-do list, and forget about. Building a brand takes time, effort, and a whole lot of consistency. You can have the most compelling story, the perfect visuals, and a well-defined voice, but if you don't show up consistently, it won't matter.

I've learned this lesson firsthand. In the early days of my business, I was inconsistent with my branding efforts. I'd post on social media sporadically, engage with my audience when I had extra time, and only focus on marketing when business was slow. The result? My audience wasn't growing, and my brand felt stagnant. It wasn't until I made a commitment to show up every single day that things started to change.

Showing up consistently doesn't mean you have to be everywhere all at once. It means making a conscious effort to be present in the spaces where your clients are. For me, that meant creating a posting schedule for Instagram, carving out time each week to engage with my followers, and staying active in my local community. It wasn't about being perfect—it was about being visible and intentional.

Consistency builds trust. When clients see you showing up day after day, it sends a powerful message: you're reliable, dedicated, and passionate about what you do. Over time, those small, consistent actions create momentum, and that momentum leads to big results. The more you invest in your brand, the more it will give back to you.

The Foundation for Your Future

Looking back, I can see how the foundation I built in those early days has shaped every aspect of my business. My brand isn't just a reflection of who I am—it's a tool that allows me to connect with clients, scale my impact, and create the kind of business and life I've always dreamed of.

When I think about where I started—juggling motherhood, self-doubt, and the chaos of building a business from scratch—I'm reminded of how far I've come. My brand has been my constant, my anchor, and my compass. It's what keeps me grounded in my values while giving me the confidence to dream bigger and reach higher.

The same can be true for you. No matter where you are in your real estate journey, you have the power to build a brand that reflects your unique story, values, and vision. It won't happen overnight, and it won't always be easy. But with clarity, consistency, and a commitment to showing up authentically, you'll create a foundation that sets you apart.

So, as you embark on this journey, remember this: Your brand isn't just what you do—it's who you are. It's the way you make people feel, the trust you build, and the legacy you leave behind. Start where you are, use what you have, and don't be afraid to dream big. The foundation you build today will support the success you create tomorrow—and the impact you leave for years to come.

TWO

Mastering Authentic Engagement

Unlocking the Heart of Connection in a Noisy World

Imagine stepping into a bustling marketplace where every vendor is shouting at the top of their lungs, each trying to outdo the other with louder pitches and flashier signs. The air is thick with noise, and it's nearly impossible to focus on any single voice. Now, picture yourself in that same market, but instead of adding to the uproar, you quietly approach someone, look them in the eye, and engage in a sincere conversation about what they're seeking. You listen intently and respond thoughtfully, and in that moment, you've made a genuine connection. That's the transformative power of authentic engagement.

In today's digital world, social media feels like a crowded marketplace where everyone's shouting to be noticed. Realtors, brands, influencers—they're all flooding our feeds with perfectly curated photos and promotional posts. But the ones who truly stand out aren't the loudest; they're the ones who focus on real connections. The ones who listen, who show up authentically, and who care more about building relationships than just making a sale.

My Journey from Broadcasting to Connecting

When I first ventured into the real estate industry, I was eager and ambitious, much like anyone starting a new chapter in their professional life. I had this notion that to be successful, I needed to be everywhere, all the time, shouting my message as loudly as possible. So, I did what many newcomers do: I filled my social media feeds with high-resolution photos of properties, detailed descriptions of listings, and occasional market statistics. I was present, but I wasn't connected.

I remember one evening when I posted what I thought was an incredible series of luxury home photos. I just knew it would grab attention—I sat back, excited, waiting for the likes, comments, and messages to pour in. But hours passed, then days, and... nothing. Barely a response. It was frustrating. Here I was, sharing some of the most beautiful properties, and it felt like no one was even noticing.

Around that time, I stumbled upon a video by Ryan Serhant, where he emphasized the importance of storytelling in real estate. He spoke about making each interaction personal and connecting with clients on a deeper level. Simultaneously, I was reading Grant Cardone's work, absorbing his insights on relentless follow-up and building trust through consistent engagement. A light bulb went off. I realized that I was so focused on showcasing properties that I had neglected the most crucial element: the people.

Determined to shift my approach, I decided to experiment. Instead of posting another property photo, I shared a story about a young couple I had recently helped find their first home. I wrote about their journey—the challenges they faced, their dreams of starting a family, and the joy we all felt when they finally held the keys to their new home. I was nervous about being so personal, but the response was overwhelming. My inbox was filled with messages from people who related to the couple's story, who thanked me for sharing something real and heartfelt.

That experience was a turning point. It taught me that people crave authenticity. They want to connect with someone who understands their aspirations and fears, someone who sees them not just as clients but as individuals with unique stories.

The Art of Speaking to One

One of the most profound lessons I've learned is the power of focusing on the individual rather than trying to appeal to the masses. In a world filled with generic messages aimed at everyone, personalization cuts through the noise and truly stands out.

Consider this: when you're scrolling through your social media feed, what captures your attention? Is it the generic advertisement blasting a one-size-fits-all message, or is it the post that speaks directly to your experiences, your challenges, and your desires? For most of us, it's the latter.

I began to envision my ideal client—a composite of the many wonderful people I've had the privilege to work with. I thought about their concerns: the anxiety of making a significant financial decision, the excitement of finding a place to call home, and the confusion over market trends. With this person in mind, I tailored my content to address their specific needs.

For instance, instead of posting a generic market update, I would write, "I know many of you are wondering if now is the right time to buy your first home, especially with all the buzz about interest rates. Let me share some insights that might help ease your worries." This approach transformed my posts from impersonal broadcasts into intimate conversations.

Ryan Serhant often emphasizes the importance of making each client feel like they're your only client. It's about giving them your undivided attention, even in a digital space. By speaking directly to one person, you create content that resonates on a deeper level, fostering trust and loyalty.

Crafting Content that Resonates

Authentic engagement is rooted in content that not only informs but also touches the heart. People remember how you make them feel more than the information you provide. Therefore, it's essential to create content that evokes emotions—be it joy, inspiration, or empathy.

I started to diversify my content, weaving in personal anecdotes, client success stories, and behind-the-scenes glimpses into my life as a realtor. I wanted my audience to see not just the professional side of me but the human side as well.

One memorable post was about a family who had to sell their home due to unforeseen circumstances. It was an emotional journey filled with tough decisions and bittersweet moments. I shared how we tackled the process together, the moments of laughter that lightened the challenges, and the sense of relief they felt when they finally found a fresh start. The post wasn't about closing a deal—it was about resilience, community, and being there for one another.

The response was incredible. People opened up about their own experiences, offering words of encouragement and solidarity. It became more than a post; it was a space for shared humanity. Inspired by this realization, I started to focus my content around three main themes that felt authentic to me and resonated with my audience:

First, there was **education**—sharing valuable tips and insights to help people feel confident and informed. Whether it was breaking down market trends, offering advice on preparing a home for sale or guiding buyers through the process, my goal was to empower my audience with the knowledge they could actually use.

Next came **inspiration**—telling real stories of transformation, resilience, and success. I loved sharing the journeys of clients who overcame challenges to find their dream homes or personal moments that showed the possibilities that come with hard work and determination. These stories weren't just about houses—they were about hope, growth, and chasing dreams.

And finally, **entertainment**—because who doesn't love a good laugh or a moment of lightness? I started posting funny behind-the-scenes moments, like mishaps during property showings, playful interactions with my team, or even just the quirks of being a working mom in real estate. It brought out my personality and added a layer of fun and relatability to my feed.

By weaving these elements together, my content became more than just posts—it became a way to truly connect with people. It wasn't about chasing likes or clicks; it was about creating a space where my audience felt informed, inspired, and entertained all at once.

Building Genuine Conversations

Engagement is a dialogue, not a monologue. It's about fostering two-way communication where both parties feel heard and valued. This means actively inviting your audience to participate and then responding thoughtfully.

I made it a point to be present and responsive. If someone took the time to comment on my post or send me a message, I ensured I replied promptly and genuinely. It wasn't just about saying "thank you" but about continuing the conversation.

For example, if someone commented, "This was really helpful, thank you!" I might respond with, "I'm so glad you found it useful! Are there any other topics you're curious about?" This approach not only shows appreciation but also encourages further engagement.

I also leveraged tools like Instagram polls and Q&A sessions. Once, I hosted a live stream where I invited followers to ask any questions they had about the home-buying process. The session was lively and interactive, and it allowed me to address real concerns in real-time.

Grant Cardone emphasizes the importance of persistence and follow-up in building relationships. I took this to heart by not just responding to comments but also checking in with past clients and followers. A simple message like, "Hey, I was thinking about you and wanted to see how things are going with your new home," can go a long way in nurturing relationships.

The Unstoppable Rise of Video

If a picture is worth a thousand words, then a video is worth a million. Video content has become a dominant force in social media engagement, offering a dynamic way to connect with your audience.

Initially, I was apprehensive about putting myself on camera. The idea of being vulnerable and potentially making mistakes in front of an audience was intimidating. However, I realized that this vulnerability is exactly what makes video content so powerful—it showcases authenticity.

My first attempt at video was a straightforward home tour. No fancy production, no professional equipment—just me and my smartphone walking through a property, pointing out features, and sharing my genuine excitement. I stumbled over my words a couple of times, laughed it off, and kept going. Honestly, I expected it to go unnoticed, but to my surprise, that simple, unpolished video got more views and engagement than anything I'd ever posted before. People commented on how approachable and real the video felt. They appreciated seeing the property through my eyes, with candid commentary rather than scripted lines.

Encouraged by this, I started incorporating more video content, which includes the following:

- **Behind-the-Scenes Moments**: Sharing snippets of my day-to-day activities, from attending property inspections to grabbing coffee between meetings.
- **Educational Segments**: Short videos explaining complex real estate concepts in simple terms.
- **Client Testimonials**: Capturing heartfelt messages from clients about their experiences.

Ryan Serhant is known for his polished yet personable video content, while Grant Cardone utilizes video to be omnipresent, reinforcing his brand continuously. Inspired by both, I aimed to create videos that were both professional and authentically me.

Cultivating a Loyal Community

Beyond individual interactions, I aspired to build a community—a space where my audience felt connected not just to me but to each other. This meant fostering an environment of support, encouragement, and shared experiences.

One initiative that resonated deeply was creating a private Facebook group for first-time homebuyers. It became a forum where members could ask questions, share their journeys, and offer advice. I facilitated discussions, provided resources, and celebrated their milestones.

I also started featuring user-generated content. With their permission, I shared stories and photos from clients who had transformed their new houses into homes. Whether it was a DIY renovation project or a garden they cultivated, these posts highlighted the joy and pride of homeownership.

Moreover, I made it a point to acknowledge and celebrate my followers' achievements. If someone commented that they had just paid off their mortgage or completed a home improvement project, I would spotlight them in my stories, applauding their efforts.

These gestures reinforced the sense of community. It wasn't just about me—it was about us.

Consistency: The Backbone of Engagement

None of these efforts would matter without consistency. Building genuine connections means showing up regularly, even on the tough days when it feels like the last thing you want to do. It's about being present and putting in the effort day after day.

Grant Cardone's 10X rule really hit home for me—it's all about giving ten times the effort to reach the success you're after. I decided to lean into that mindset, committing to a regular schedule for creating content and engaging with my audience. It wasn't always easy, but the consistency made all the difference.

I developed a content calendar to plan my posts in advance, ensuring a balanced mix of educational, inspirational, and entertaining content. This organization allowed me to stay on track and maintain a steady presence.

Furthermore, I set aside dedicated time each day to interact with my audience. Whether it was during my morning coffee or in the evening after showings, I made engagement a non-negotiable part of my routine.

Tracking metrics also played a crucial role. By analyzing which posts garnered the most engagement, I could refine my content strategy to better serve my audience's interests.

Embracing Authenticity Over Perfection

Perhaps the most significant shift in my approach was letting go of the need for perfection. In the past, I hesitated to share content unless it was meticulously crafted. However, I learned that people resonate more with authenticity than with flawlessness.

I remember a time when I was gearing up to host a live Q&A session, feeling prepared and ready to go, when out of nowhere, my dog started barking like crazy. For a split second, I thought about postponing—it felt so unprofessional. But instead, I decided to roll with it and introduced my furry little chaos-maker to the audience. What could've been a stressful moment turned into something unexpectedly heartwarming. People loved it. It made me more relatable, brought some laughs, and reminded me that authenticity—even in imperfect moments—can be incredibly powerful. Embracing imperfections allowed me to connect on a more genuine level. It showed that I'm not just a professional but a person with quirks and real-life challenges, just like everyone else.

The Ripple Effect of Authentic Engagement

The impact of mastering authentic engagement extends beyond social media metrics. It translates into tangible results—stronger client relationships, increased referrals, and a reputation built on trust.

One of the most rewarding outcomes was when a client told me, "I felt like I already knew you before we even met in person." They had followed my content for months, and our initial meeting felt less like a formal consultation and more like catching up with a friend.

Another client, who was initially hesitant about the buying process, shared that my educational videos empowered them to take the leap. They appreciated the clarity and honesty I provided, which alleviated their fears.

These experiences reaffirmed that authentic engagement isn't just a marketing strategy—it's a means of making a meaningful difference in people's lives.

Key Takeaways

- **Focus on the Individual**: Tailor your content to speak directly to your ideal client's needs and aspirations.
- **Evoke Emotion Through Storytelling**: Share narratives that resonate on a personal level, fostering deeper connections.
- **Foster Genuine Conversations**: Engage actively with your audience, transforming interactions into relationships.
- **Leverage Video for Authenticity**: Utilize video content to showcase your personality and connect dynamically.
- **Build Community**: Create spaces where your audience feels connected, supported, and valued.

- **Be Consistent and Present**: Commit to regular engagement, showing up authentically every day.
- **Embrace Imperfection**: Let go of the need for perfection and allow your true self to shine through.

Moving Forward: Your Journey to Authentic Engagement

Mastering authentic engagement is an ongoing journey, one that requires introspection, adaptability, and genuine care for your audience. It's about shifting from a mindset of selling to one of serving.

As you step onto this path, remember that authenticity isn't a strategy or a box to check—it's a way of living and working. It's about aligning your professional persona with who you truly are, letting your values and personality shine through in every interaction. When you lead with authenticity, you're not just building a business—you're building trust, connection, and lasting relationships.

Take inspiration from industry icons like Ryan Serhant and Grant Cardone, but don't try to copy their playbook. The magic lies in forging your own path, one that reflects your story, your experiences, and your unique voice. These are the things that make you stand out, that make people gravitate toward you.

At the end of the day, people won't remember every listing you shared or every statistic you posted. What they will remember is how you made them feel—the trust you earned, the support you gave, and the way you showed up with genuine care and purpose.

So, as you step into the crowded, noisy marketplace, don't aim to just be another voice in the mix. Be the one who truly listens, who engages meaningfully, and who creates real connections. That's how you stand out, make an impact, and leave a lasting impression—one person, one relationship, and one moment at a time.

THREE

Identifying and Targeting Your Ideal Audience

When I first became a realtor, I thought success meant saying yes to every opportunity. If someone called about a rental 50 miles away, I was there. If a lead wanted to look at 20 houses on a Saturday, I made it happen—even if I knew they were just "window shopping." I believed that casting the widest net possible was the key to success. But here's the thing: it left me exhausted, scattered, and honestly, feeling like I was failing.

Then, one day, I had a breakthrough. I was working with a young family who had recently relocated to the area. They were looking for a home where their kids could grow up with plenty of space to explore—a place that felt like more than just a house. It reminded me of my own story, living on land with my family and finding joy in the simple, beautiful moments. I poured my heart into helping them, and when they found their dream home, I realized something important: these were the clients I was meant to serve.

From that moment on, I stopped trying to appeal to everyone and started focusing on the clients who aligned with my values, passions, and strengths. My business didn't just grow—it flourished. And the best part? I loved every minute of it.

Finding Your People

Every realtor has a unique story, and that story naturally draws in the right people—if you let it. For me, my story is about family, community, and the beauty of creating a home. That's why I gravitate toward clients who value those same things. They're the ones who light up when I talk about the local schools, the charm of a neighborhood festival, or the quiet joy of waking up to a sunrise over an open field.

When you're clear about who you want to serve, everything changes. Your marketing feels more authentic. Your conversations feel more natural. And your clients feel like they've found the perfect match.

What Do Your Dream Clients Look Like?

Imagine them walking through the door. Are they young professionals buying their first condo in the city? Families searching for their forever home? Retirees downsizing to something cozy and manageable? Picture them in vivid detail: their goals, their struggles, and what they're hoping to find.

I remember one family in particular—a couple with three kids and two golden retrievers. They wanted a home with enough room for everyone to have their own space, but their dream was a backyard big enough for the kids to play soccer and for the dogs to run freely. As they described their vision, I could see it so clearly in my mind. That clarity helped me focus my search, and when we found the perfect property, it felt like magic—for all of us.

Embracing Your Niche

Here's a little secret: You don't have to be everything to everyone. In fact, the more specific you are about what you do and who you serve, the more successful you'll be. For me, it's equestrian properties, luxury homes, and land sales. Those niches align with my passions and my expertise, and they allow me to stand out in a crowded market.

At first, I worried about turning people away. Would I miss out on opportunities by narrowing my focus? But what I found was the opposite: By owning my niche, I became the go-to expert in those areas. People didn't just call me because I was a realtor—they called me because they knew I understood their unique needs.

Walking in Their Shoes

One of the most powerful things you can do in real estate—or in any business—is to truly step into your client's shoes. What are they feeling as they scroll through listings late at night? Is it excitement, imagining their future in a new space? Or is it overwhelm, wondering how they'll ever navigate the process? Maybe it's a little bit of both. When you take the time to understand their emotions, you can connect with them on a deeper, more personal level.

I'll never forget working with one particular couple. They were first-time buyers who had spent years saving every penny to purchase their dream home. This wasn't just a transaction for them—it was the culmination of years of hard work and sacrifice. Every decision felt monumental, from choosing the right neighborhood to picking the shade of paint for the living room. They worried about every detail and hesitated to make the wrong choice.

Instead of rushing them or trying to steer the process, I leaned into their experience. I took the time to listen to their concerns, to answer their late-night texts filled with "what-ifs," and to celebrate every small milestone with them. I treated their journey like it was just as important to me as it was to them—because it was. By the time they signed the papers and got the keys, they weren't just clients—they were friends. Helping them wasn't just about finding the right house; it was about helping them start a new chapter of their lives.

Walking in your client's shoes isn't just about empathy—it's about creating an experience that feels personalized and meaningful. When people feel seen, heard, and valued, they don't just see you as their agent; they see you as someone who truly cares about their journey.

Speaking Their Language

Understanding your audience means being able to speak directly to them in a way that feels personal and relatable. It's not about throwing around industry jargon or trying to sound overly polished. It's about meeting your clients where they are and showing them that you get it—you understand their needs, their dreams, and even their fears.

For me, that means keeping my tone warm, approachable, and real. My conversations aren't just about square footage or market trends—they're about what really matters to people. I talk about the things that make a house a home: a kitchen big enough for family dinners, a backyard perfect for summer barbecues, or a quiet corner that's just right for a home office.

I remember working with a family who was relocating for a new job. Their kids were nervous about leaving their school and friends behind. Instead of focusing solely on the logistics of the move, I made it a priority to find a neighborhood where their kids could thrive—close to good schools, parks, and other families. It wasn't just about the house; it was about creating a sense of belonging.

Your voice should reflect who you are and resonate with the people you want to attract. If you're someone who loves diving into the numbers and explaining market data, let that shine. If you're the patient, hand-holding type who reassures first-time buyers every step of the way, own that. The beauty of real estate is that there's room for every style. The key is to be consistent and authentic so the people you connect with know exactly who you are and what you stand for.

When you speak your clients' language, you're not just selling houses—you're building relationships. And those relationships? They're the foundation of a business that lasts.

Building Relationships That Last

Real estate isn't just about transactions—it's about relationships. Some of my most rewarding experiences have come from working with families who trust me enough to come back years later when they're ready for their next chapter. That trust is built through consistency, authenticity, and showing up for them—even after the sale is done.

For example, I keep in touch with clients through handwritten notes, holiday cards, and even texts to say, "I was thinking about you today—how's the house?" Those small gestures remind them that I care, not just about their business, but about their lives.

What's Your Next Step?

Take a moment to reflect on the clients you've loved working with the most. What made those relationships special? What did you enjoy about the process? Use those insights to guide your next steps. Remember, the goal isn't to work with everyone—it's to work with the right ones.

FOUR

Platform-Specific Strategies for Realtors

When I first started using social media for real estate, I felt like I was trying to learn a foreign language. Instagram, Facebook, TikTok—each platform seemed to have its own rules, and I wasn't sure how to navigate any of them. I'd sit at my kitchen table at night, scrolling through other people's posts, trying to figure out how they made it look so effortless. Meanwhile, my youngest was running around the house looking for her favorite stuffed animal, and my coffee was getting cold. I couldn't help but think, *How am I supposed to keep up with all of this?*

I eventually realized that social media wasn't about doing it perfectly. It was about doing it authentically. Instead of trying to be everywhere or copy what others were doing, I focused on showing up as myself—messy bun, coffee in hand, and all. That shift changed everything. Social media became less about algorithms and more about building real connections. And it worked. Over time, each platform became a space for me to share a different side of my business and personality, and in doing so, I found my rhythm.

Instagram: Where Stories Shine

Instagram quickly became one of my favorite platforms. It's like a digital scrapbook—a place where I can share the highs, the struggles, and everything in between. For me, Instagram isn't just about selling houses; it's about sharing the heart and hustle of my real estate life.

I remember one day in particular. I had spent the morning staging a home, running between rooms with my hair in a messy bun and a latte glued to my hand. By the time I was done, the living room looked like something out of a magazine. Instead of overthinking it, I snapped a quick photo and posted it to my Stories with the caption, *"Real estate reality: coffee in one hand, a sofa throw in the other!"* The response was instant. People loved seeing the behind-the-scenes chaos that made the final product look so polished.

One of my most memorable posts was a photo of my daughter running across the yard at one of my listings. I captioned it, *"A home is so much more than four walls—it's where memories are made."* That post didn't just get likes; it sparked conversations. People messaged me to share their own stories about what "home" meant to them. That's the beauty of Instagram. It's not just about showing what you do; it's about connecting with people on a deeper level.

Instagram Stories became my favorite way to share my day-to-day life. Whether I was showing homes, grabbing coffee with a client, or just catching a quiet moment on my family farm, Stories allowed me to let people in. My Reels, on the other hand, became a way to have fun while educating my audience. I'd create short clips like *"5 Signs You're Ready to Buy"* or quick property tours set to trending music. And my feed? It's a mix of professional updates and personal moments. I've found that the posts people love the most are the ones that feel real—not overly polished, but true to who I am.

Facebook: Community at Its Heart

For me, Facebook feels like home. It's where I connect with families, friends, and neighbors—and where many of my clients spend their time. Unlike Instagram, which is all about visuals, Facebook is about stories, conversations, and creating a sense of community.

I'll never forget the day I realized just how powerful Facebook could be. Someone posted in a local community group asking, *"Who's a good realtor in the area?"* Before I even had the chance to respond, six people tagged me. That moment was such a confidence boost. It reminded me that being active and engaged in my community—both online and offline—wasn't just about visibility; it was about building trust.

One of my favorite ways to use Facebook is to share little moments from my community. I'll post a picture of a new bakery that just opened or give a shout-out to a local coffee shop. I also love highlighting upcoming events, like farmers' markets or holiday parades. These posts aren't about selling anything—they're about showing people that I'm invested in the place we all call home.

Then there are the live videos. I'll admit, going live used to make me nervous. What if I said the wrong thing? What if no one watched? But once I started, I realized how much people loved real-time interaction. Whether I'm walking through a new listing, answering questions about the market, or just chatting about my favorite neighborhoods, going live has become one of my favorite ways to connect.

LinkedIn: Polished but Personal

LinkedIn used to feel like a platform on which I didn't belong. It seemed too corporate, like I had to present this perfect, polished version of myself that didn't leave room for personality. However, once I started using LinkedIn as a space to share my insights and connect with other professionals, I realized how valuable it could be.

One of my most rewarding LinkedIn posts was about helping a family relocate for a new job. I shared the story of how we found a home that balanced their commute with their kids' school district, and I talked about the challenges and triumphs along the way. That post resonated with so many people, especially professionals who were navigating their own relocations. It even led to referrals from HR reps and relocation specialists who appreciated my approach.

For me, LinkedIn is about striking the right balance between professional and personal. I'll write thoughtful posts about market trends or share articles on the real estate industry, but I also make room for stories that highlight the human side of my work. It's not just about showcasing what I know—it's about showing who I am.

TikTok: Fun and Unexpected

When I first heard about TikTok, I thought, *There's no way this is for me.* I couldn't imagine myself dancing in front of the camera or lip-syncing to viral sounds. But after watching a few real estate TikToks, I decided to give it a shot—and I was hooked.

One of my first TikToks was a behind-the-scenes clip of me struggling to open a stubborn lockbox. I captioned it, *"The glamorous life of a realtor."* It was silly, unpolished, and completely relatable—and it got more views than I ever expected. That's when I realized that TikTok wasn't about perfection; it was about personality.

Now, I use TikTok to share everything from quick home-buying tips to funny moments from my day. I love hopping on trends and putting a real estate spin on them, but my favorite videos are the ones that feel uniquely me. TikTok has given me a space to let loose, have fun, and show a side of myself that people might not see on other platforms.

Your Social Media Game Plan

Every platform has its own strengths, but the key is finding what works for you. For me, social media isn't just a marketing tool—it's a way to build real connections. Whether it's sharing a heartwarming story on Instagram, posting about a local event on Facebook, or having fun with a trend on TikTok, every interaction is an opportunity to build trust and start a conversation.

The truth is, social media doesn't have to be perfect. It just has to be authentic. When you show up as yourself, people notice—and that's where the magic happens.

FIVE

Content Creation and Curation Mastery

I'll never forget the first time someone said, "I feel like I already know you from your posts!" It was a client who'd been following me on social media for months before reaching out. They told me they loved how I made real estate feel approachable and fun, and how my posts always gave off the vibe that I truly cared about my clients.

That moment stuck with me because it reminded me of something powerful: content isn't just about what you post—it's about how it makes people feel. Every post, video, or story is an opportunity to show people who you are and why they should trust you.

When I started treating my content like a conversation instead of a sales pitch, everything changed. My audience grew, my engagement skyrocketed, and most importantly, the right people started reaching out. That's when I realized that great content isn't just about marketing—it's about connection.

Creating Content That Feels Like You

Your content should feel like an extension of who you are. It's your personality, your values, your quirks—everything that makes you *you*. Early on, I thought I needed to look like the real estate agents I saw online: perfectly polished, flawless photos, and captions that sounded like they came straight out of a marketing textbook. But the more I tried to fit into that mold, the less connected I felt to my own content—and to my audience.

Then, one day, I posted a photo that wasn't polished at all. It was a candid shot of my husband and daughter riding in the combine during harvest season. I captioned it, *"This is why I do what I do. Every late-night email, every showing, every closing—it's all for them."* That post wasn't about real estate, but it sparked something. People commented, shared their own stories, and sent me messages saying it inspired them. It was a lightbulb moment: people don't just want to see your business—they want to see *you*.

That's when I realized that the best content doesn't come from trying to be perfect. It comes from being real. Sure, I still post beautiful listing photos and market updates, but I also share the chaos of being a working mom, life on the farm, and those small, unfiltered moments that make life beautiful.

The Power of Education

When I started creating content, I had this nagging fear of sounding too "salesy." I didn't want people to feel like I was just trying to push listings or brag about my business. But the more I thought about it, the more I realized that real estate isn't just about selling—it's about helping people. And one of the best ways to help people is by teaching them.

Think about it: buying or selling a home is one of the biggest decisions most people will ever make. It's exciting, but it's also overwhelming. There's so much to learn, and that's where we, as realtors, can step in. Educational content isn't just about sharing information—it's about empowering people to make confident, informed decisions.

One of my most popular posts was a simple video titled *"5 Questions to Ask Your Realtor Before Listing Your Home."* I filmed it in my car after a meeting, speaking directly to the camera. It wasn't rehearsed or scripted, but it was honest and full of practical advice. The response blew me away. People commented things like, *"I wish I'd known this before I sold my house!"* and *"This is so helpful—thank you!"* That post reminded me that sometimes, the most valuable thing you can share is your knowledge.

Educational content doesn't have to be complicated. It can be a short video explaining what "under contract" means, a post breaking down the biggest mistakes first-time buyers make, or even a quick tip about staging a home. The key is to keep it simple, relatable, and focused on what your audience actually wants to know.

And here's the best part: when you share valuable information, you're not just helping people—you're showing them that you're an expert who truly cares about their success. That's the kind of trust that turns followers into clients.

Mixing Up Your Content

When it comes to creating content, variety is everything. Imagine walking into a restaurant and finding that the only thing on the menu is chicken. Sure, chicken's great, but after a while, it gets boring. The same goes for your social media feed. If you're only posting listing photos or market updates, you're missing a huge opportunity to engage your audience on a deeper level.

I like to think of my content as a well-balanced plate. A little storytelling here, a dash of education there, a sprinkle of inspiration, and just the right amount of entertainment. Each type of content serves a different purpose, but together, they create a full picture of who I am and what I bring to the table.

Storytelling is my favorite ingredient. It's where I share the moments that make real estate feel personal, like helping a family find their dream home or the time a client cried happy tears at closing. One story that stands out is about a couple who were buying their first home after years of saving. I posted a photo of them holding their keys with the caption, *"This moment makes every late night and early morning worth it."* That post didn't just celebrate their milestone—it celebrated why I love what I do.

Education is my way of adding value. I'll share tips for first-time buyers, explain how to navigate a bidding war, or demystify confusing terms like "earnest money." These posts aren't flashy, but they're incredibly impactful because they show my audience that I'm here to help.

Inspiration is about sharing the big-picture stuff—the moments that remind us why we do what we do. Sometimes, it's a quote that motivates me. Other times, it's a personal reflection, like celebrating a client's journey or looking back on how far I've come in my career. Inspiration doesn't just attract people—it builds loyalty.

And then there's **entertainment**—the lighthearted, funny, and sometimes downright goofy side of real estate. Whether it's a behind-the-scenes look at staging a home, a meme that perfectly sums up the market, or a TikTok trend with a real estate twist, entertainment adds a human element to your content. People want to laugh, and when you make them smile, they're more likely to stick around.

Curation: Sharing the Spotlight

Creating content isn't just about what you post—it's also about what you share. Highlighting others, whether it's a local business, a community event, or a client's story, shows that you're invested in more than just yourself.

One of my favorite examples of curation was when I helped a family find their dream home. After closing, they posted a photo of themselves in front of the house, holding the keys and beaming with pride. They tagged me in the post, and I reshared it on my feed with the caption, *"This is what it's all about. Congratulations to the Johnson family on finding your forever home!"* The response was incredible. People love seeing real moments and genuine happiness—it's a reminder of the impact we make as realtors.

Curation also means shining a spotlight on the community. I'll post about a new coffee shop opening, share details about a local festival, or highlight a small business I love. These posts aren't about me—they're about celebrating the people and places that make my community special. And in doing so, they show my audience that I'm not just a realtor—I'm a neighbor who cares.

Consistency Is Key

If there's one thing I've learned about content creation, it's that consistency is everything. Showing up once in a while isn't enough. To build trust, stay top of mind, and truly connect with your audience, you have to show up regularly—especially on the days when you don't feel like it.

There have been plenty of times when I've felt too tired, too busy, or just uninspired to post. But then I remind myself why I started this journey in the first place. Every post is an opportunity to connect with someone who might need what I have to offer, whether it's a first-time buyer feeling overwhelmed or a family searching for their forever home.

For me, consistency isn't about being perfect—it's about being present. Some days, that looks like a polished Reel or a carefully crafted caption. On other days, it's a quick Story of me juggling work and family life. The point is to keep showing up, because when you do, people notice. And over time, those small, consistent efforts add up to something big.

Learning as You Go

If you were to scroll back to my first few posts, you'd probably laugh. I know I do. The photos were grainy, the captions were awkward, and I had no idea what I was doing. But here's the thing: none of that mattered. What mattered was that I started.

Content creation is a journey, not a destination. You don't have to be an expert on day one—you just have to be willing to show up, experiment, and learn as you go. Some posts will flop, and that's okay. Every misstep is a chance to improve, and every success is a reminder that you're on the right track.

At the end of the day, the most important thing isn't what you post—it's how you make people feel. When you create content that feels like you, it resonates. It builds trust, inspires connection, and turns followers into clients. And that's what makes it all worth it.

SIX

Building and Nurturing a Brand Community

Imagine a close-knit neighborhood where everyone knows each other by name, sharing a true sense of belonging. This is what I aim to create in my brand's digital community—a space where clients, followers, and friends feel like they're part of something more than just a transaction. As a realtor, I've seen firsthand how much people crave spaces where they can connect over shared values, experiences, and goals. Creating this type of community transforms your brand from simply a service provider into a trusted partner, confidante, and ally.

The foundation of a thriving community begins with a clear purpose and values that resonate. For me, that purpose is about more than buying or selling homes; it's about building a space for people to exchange advice, support, and inspiration. I see my community as a place where first-time buyers, experienced investors, and everyone in between can connect, share their journeys, and feel uplifted. Having a mission that's simple and heartfelt—a mission centered around support, transparency, and community—gives everyone in the group a sense of shared purpose. Defining core values like inclusivity, respect, and encouragement ensures that all interactions align with this vision, creating a positive atmosphere where people feel truly welcome.

Choosing the right platform for your community is essential. In my business, I've found that Facebook Groups are a great space for my community to interact, especially for sharing tips, asking questions, and joining local conversations. Platforms like Mighty Networks or Slack are also worth exploring for more customized experiences, particularly if you want to create a more private or intimate space. When selecting a platform, I think about the group's purpose and whether a public or private space is best. A public space can help reach a wider audience, but a private group can foster those deeper, more meaningful connections that make members feel like part of an exclusive group—one that has their back.

Establishing clear community guidelines is crucial for building a welcoming culture. When setting up my community's rules, I focused on keeping things simple yet clear, emphasizing respect and inclusivity. I encourage members to share their experiences, ask questions, and support one another. These guidelines not only create a safe space but also set the tone for how members interact. By prioritizing respect and genuine connection, we build a community where everyone feels valued and empowered to contribute, creating stronger bonds and a more resilient group.

Consistent, meaningful engagement is the heartbeat of any vibrant community. Regular interactions keep members connected and make them feel like they're part of something dynamic and responsive. I host virtual meetups, where members can ask questions, share their home-buying journeys, or simply connect. Creating discussion threads on trending topics also brings people together, allowing them to exchange ideas and insights. By fostering these touchpoints, I keep the community lively and engaging, allowing members to feel that their voices matter and that they're part of a supportive network.

Exercise: Craft Your Community's Mission Statement

Dedicate time to reflect on the purpose and values you envision for your brand community. Think about what makes your community unique and the core values you wish to uphold. Draft a mission statement that encapsulates these elements, ensuring it is concise yet inspirational. Share this draft with a few trusted colleagues or community members for feedback. Use their insights to refine your statement, making sure it resonates with your audience and sets a clear direction for your community's future interactions. This exercise will help solidify your community's foundation, guiding its growth and evolution.

By defining a purpose, choosing the right platform, setting guidelines, and fostering consistent engagement, you can create a brand community that feels like home. It's about creating a place where members feel seen, heard, and supported—a place that represents more than just business, but a shared journey toward connection and success.

Encouraging Community Participation

In the world of brand communities, encouraging active participation is key to building a strong, engaged group. When community members feel involved and valued, they're more likely to contribute meaningfully. One effective way to inspire engagement is by launching community challenges and contests. These initiatives add a sense of excitement and fun, sparking participation and creativity. Imagine organizing a contest where members share their most creative real estate staging ideas or photos of their favorite neighborhood spots. Offering rewards or recognition to top contributors can further motivate members, creating an energetic atmosphere that fosters connection. When people see their contributions highlighted, they feel valued, driving even more engagement and deepening community bonds.

Encouraging user-generated content is another powerful way to boost engagement. By inviting members to share their stories and experiences, you tap into the diverse knowledge and perspectives within your community. For instance, ask members to share success stories from their home-buying journey or insights on local market trends. Featuring this member-created content on your brand's channels not only showcases the diversity of your community but also builds a sense of ownership among members. This recognition strengthens their connection to the community and inspires others to contribute, weaving together a rich tapestry of voices and ideas.

Facilitating collaborative projects and events is a dynamic way to unite community members around common goals. These initiatives can range from planning group projects, like local charity events, to organizing collaborative content creation sessions. For example, a community might come together to host a neighborhood clean-up, with members pitching in their time and skills. These group efforts don't just strengthen bonds among members—they align the community with broader social goals, giving it a sense of purpose and positive impact. Collaborative content creation sessions, where members brainstorm and produce content together, can also inspire creativity and innovation. These shared projects help reinforce the community's cohesion and vitality.

Recognizing and celebrating the efforts of active community members is essential for maintaining a vibrant, engaged group. Acknowledging members' contributions boosts their morale and sets an example for others. Highlighting achievements in newsletters or community updates is a great way to showcase their involvement. This could range from spotlight features for members who have made a big impact to shout-outs for those who actively participate in discussions. Celebrating these contributions creates a culture of appreciation and motivation, where everyone feels their efforts are valued. Many successful brands showcase member achievements, creating spaces to honor contributions and foster a sense of pride within the community.

Harnessing the Power of Social Proof

Imagine walking into a cozy café, filled with people chatting and enjoying their favorite drinks. You overhear someone praising the barista for crafting the perfect latte, and suddenly, you feel compelled to try the same. This is social proof in action—when we look to others for guidance on what to do. In the digital world, testimonials and reviews play a similar role, especially in real estate. By showcasing positive feedback from satisfied clients, you boost your brand's credibility. Feature these testimonials on social media platforms where potential clients are likely to spend time. A heartfelt story from a happy homeowner who found their dream property through your agency speaks volumes. Additionally, consider creating a dedicated testimonials page on your website, highlighting these success stories as a living portfolio that builds trust with new clients.

Encouraging word-of-mouth referrals is another powerful way to leverage social proof. When clients and community members speak highly of your brand, it validates their experience and encourages others to engage. Implement referral programs with attractive incentives to motivate members to share their experiences with friends and family. You could offer a discount or a small gift for every successful referral. Sharing these referral success stories within the community not only celebrates the referrer but also showcases the benefits of the program, creating a cycle of trust and engagement. This approach builds loyalty while naturally expanding your brand's reach.

Highlighting client success stories and case studies provides a deeper view into the impact of your services. These stories go beyond testimonials by detailing how you helped solve specific client challenges. Consider writing in-depth case studies that showcase the journey of clients who achieved notable success through your services, outlining the challenges faced, solutions provided, and the results. Adding video testimonials brings an extra layer of authenticity, capturing emotions that written words can't always convey. By sharing these stories, you reinforce your brand's credibility and showcase the real value you offer.

Working with community influencers can further amplify social proof. Influencers, respected by their followers, can introduce your brand to a broader audience. Partner with local influencers whose values align with yours, creating content that highlights your services or offers a guided property tour narrated by the influencer. Their endorsement brings credibility, attracting potential clients who trust their recommendations. Featuring these testimonials on your platforms extends their reach and helps you connect with an audience who relates to the influencer's lifestyle, creating an authentic bridge between your brand and new clients can drive your brand forward.

SEVEN

Building an Irresistible Personal Brand

When I first stepped into the world of real estate, "branding" wasn't even in my vocabulary. I thought success would come purely from hard work—helping families find homes, getting a few referrals, and letting the results speak for themselves. But it didn't take long to realize that being great at what you do isn't enough. People need to know who you are, feel connected to you, and trust you before they'll ever reach out.

The turning point for me came when a couple said, *"We've been following you for months, and we just knew you were the right person to help us."* They didn't mention my sales stats or my certifications. They didn't care about how many homes I'd sold. What stood out to them was the way I showed up—sharing bits of my life, my personality, and my passion for helping people. That moment was a revelation: your personal brand is what draws the right clients to you, long before you even meet them.

What Makes a Brand Irresistible?

An irresistible brand isn't about having a fancy logo or a perfectly curated website. It's about creating a feeling—a sense of trust, connection, and relatability that makes people say, *"I want to work with them."*

Early in my career, I thought I had to project this super-polished, hyper-professional image to be taken seriously. I wore blazers to every showing, wrote stiff, formal emails, and avoided sharing anything personal. But the truth? It felt exhausting, and it wasn't me.

Everything changed when I started leaning into my real self. Instead of trying to impress, I focused on connecting. I started sharing stories about life on the farm, the challenges of balancing work and motherhood, and my genuine love for helping families find homes. Suddenly, people weren't just interested in my services—they were drawn to my story, my authenticity, and my approachability.

An irresistible brand is about being unapologetically *you*. It's about showing people your values, your personality, and what you stand for—not what you think they want to see.

Define Your Brand Pillars

Think of your brand as a house, and your brand pillars are the foundation that holds it all together. Without a strong foundation, everything else can feel scattered or inconsistent. For me, defining my pillars was a process of self-discovery. I asked myself: *What do I care about most? What drives me?* The answers became clear: authenticity, family, and empowerment.

These pillars guide everything I do, from how I interact with clients to the type of content I share. I'll never forget a young couple I worked with early on. They were first-time buyers, completely overwhelmed by the process and unsure if they could even afford a home. Instead of rushing them or bombarding them with information, I slowed down. I broke everything into simple steps, celebrated their wins, and stayed patient through their anxieties. When they got their keys, they said, *"We couldn't have done this without you."*

That moment reminded me why I do what I do. It's not just about closing deals; it's about walking alongside people during some of the most emotional and important decisions of their lives. My pillars—authenticity, family, and empowerment—aren't just words. They're the compass that keeps me grounded in everything I do.

If you're not sure what your pillars are, start by asking yourself: *What do I want people to remember about me? What values guide me every day?* Your pillars should reflect not just your professional mission but your personal beliefs too.

Be Unmistakably You

For years, I thought blending in was the way to succeed. I tried to appeal to everyone, thinking that being "neutral" would make me approachable. But as I've learned, trying to be everything to everyone makes you forgettable.

The real magic happens when you lean into what makes you unique. For me, it's the duality of being a no-nonsense realtor and a small-town mom who loves farm life. That's why I don't shy away from posting about my kids, the chaos of mornings on the farm, or even the occasional workday mishap.

One post that stands out in my memory was about running late to a showing because my toddler spilled juice all over my outfit. I hesitated to share it because I thought it might seem unprofessional. But when I finally hit "post," the response was incredible. People commented, *"This is so relatable!"* and *"Thanks for keeping it real!"* That post got more engagement than any perfectly polished listing photo I'd ever shared.

Being unmistakably you means showing your quirks, your imperfections, and your personality. Those are the things people remember —and in real estate, being memorable is everything.

Tell Your Story

Everyone loves a good story. Your personal journey isn't just a part of your brand—it's the heart of it. Your story is what makes you relatable and sets you apart from the competition.

For me, my story starts with resilience. After my divorce, I found myself starting over from scratch, with no roadmap or safety net. Real estate wasn't just a career choice—it was a way to build a better life for my kids. Every step of my journey, from juggling showings with school drop-offs to celebrating my first big sale, is a part of the story that brought me here.

Sharing my story has opened doors I never expected. It's helped clients see that I'm not just a realtor—I'm someone who's been through challenges and come out stronger. But your story doesn't have to be dramatic or perfectly crafted to make an impact. It just has to be *yours*.

What are the pivotal moments that shaped your journey? What lessons have you learned along the way? When you share those experiences, you invite people to connect with you on a deeper level.

Consistency is Everything

One of the hardest lessons I've learned is the importance of consistency. Early on, I'd post whenever I felt inspired—sometimes every day, sometimes not for weeks. Unsurprisingly, my audience wasn't growing. Then, I committed to showing up regularly, whether it was posting on social media, sending follow-up emails, or staying active in my community. The difference was immediate.

Consistency doesn't mean you have to be on every platform or post every single day. It's about reliability. It's about showing up in ways that feel sustainable for you and valuable for your audience.

For me, consistency looks like sharing weekly updates about the market, staying engaged in local events, and regularly connecting with past clients. It's not about perfection—it's about building trust over time.

Leverage Your Visual Identity

Your visual identity is often the first impression people have of your brand. It's not just about looking polished—it's about creating a cohesive and authentic representation of who you are.

When I started building my brand, I invested in professional headshots and worked with a designer to create a simple, elegant logo. But my favorite visual content is the candid moments—the photos of my kids playing on the farm, a snap of me in action during a showing, or even a quick selfie from a community event. These visuals are a reminder that while I take my work seriously, I don't take myself too seriously.

A strong visual identity doesn't have to be expensive or flashy. It just has to feel like *you*.

Final Thoughts on Building Your Brand

Building a personal brand isn't about creating a version of yourself that you think people want to see. It's about uncovering who you already are and sharing that with the world. Your brand is the reflection of your values, your journey, and the impact you want to make.

When you define your pillars, share your story, and consistently show up as your authentic self, you create a brand that people can't help but be drawn to. It's not about being perfect—it's about being real. And in an industry built on trust, that's what makes all the difference.

EIGHT

Scaling Your Presence for Exponential Growth

I'll never forget the time I walked into a local coffee shop to grab my usual morning latte. As I waited in line, a woman turned to me and said, *"Aren't you Randi? I've seen your videos about the real estate market, and I love how you explain things so clearly."*

At first, I was caught off guard. She wasn't a client or someone I'd ever met before, yet she spoke to me like she already knew me. Then it clicked—this was the ripple effect of all the hours I'd spent building my presence online. Through my videos, posts, and consistent messaging, I'd become more than a realtor; I'd become someone people trusted, even before meeting me in person.

That's the beauty of scaling your presence. It's not just about visibility—it's about creating meaningful connections at scale. It's about showing up in ways that resonate, building trust with people you've never met, and ensuring that when someone thinks about real estate, your name is the first that comes to mind.

Think Bigger, Act Bigger

When I first started in real estate, I thought small. I focused on the next client, the next transaction, and the next paycheck. It wasn't until I shifted my mindset that I started seeing exponential growth. Instead of thinking of myself as "just a realtor," I began to see myself as a brand. Instead of focusing solely on sales, I started thinking about relationships, impact, and the legacy I wanted to build.

This shift didn't happen overnight. It started with small changes, like envisioning how each transaction could lead to referrals or how a single piece of content could spark multiple conversations. I began asking myself questions like, *How can this one action ripple outward? How can I make a bigger impact with less effort?*

One of the most transformative moments came when I decided to treat my social media as an extension of my business rather than an afterthought. I stopped thinking of posts as "extras" and started seeing them as opportunities to create lasting impressions. Instead of just sharing listings, I leaned into storytelling, education, and connection.

When you think bigger, you naturally start to act bigger. You stop comparing yourself to others and focus on your own unique strengths. You invest in tools that amplify your reach, and you build systems that allow you to scale without burning out.

The Power of Video

I used to shy away from video because I was afraid of putting myself out there. I didn't like the sound of my voice, and I worried about looking awkward. But deep down, I knew video was non-negotiable. It's one of the most powerful ways to connect with people at scale. It lets you show your personality, share your expertise, and build trust in a way that static posts just can't.

My first attempt at video wasn't perfect. I filmed a walkthrough of a property with my phone, and let's just say my nerves showed. I tripped over my words, forgot half of what I wanted to say, and ended up laughing at myself halfway through. But here's the thing: people loved it. They didn't care that it wasn't polished. What they saw was someone genuine, enthusiastic, and passionate about what they do.

Now, video is a cornerstone of my business. Whether I'm sharing a market update, walking through a property, or showing the "day in the life" of a realtor, video allows me to connect with my audience on a deeper level. It's not about being perfect—it's about being present and real.

One of the most impactful videos I ever posted was a short clip about the three biggest mistakes first-time buyers make. It was simple, straight to the point, and packed with value. That one video sparked dozens of messages, new leads, and even a referral from someone I'd never worked with before.

If you're nervous about getting started, start small. Record a quick Instagram Story, film a one-minute tip, or go live for just five minutes. The more you do it, the easier it gets. And the results? They're worth every moment of discomfort.

Build a Content Ecosystem

For a long time, I felt overwhelmed by the idea of creating more content. Between showings, contracts, and family responsibilities, it felt like there just wasn't enough time. But then I discovered the concept of a content ecosystem, and it changed everything.

Here's how it works: Start with one core piece of content. For example, let's say I record a video about the top three trends in today's housing market. That video becomes the centerpiece. From there, I can break it down into smaller pieces—a blog post for my website, short clips for Instagram Reels, a carousel post for LinkedIn, and a quick tip for TikTok.

By repurposing content, I'm able to stay consistent without constantly reinventing the wheel. It also reinforces my message. Someone might watch the full video on YouTube, see a snippet of it on Instagram, and read a related post on LinkedIn. That repetition builds trust and keeps me top of mind.

The key to a successful content ecosystem is planning. I dedicate one day a week to brainstorming, filming, and creating. By batching my efforts, I'm able to produce more content in less time—and with far less stress.

Expand Your Platform Strategy

When I first started using social media, I poured all my energy into Instagram. It was comfortable, and it worked—for a while. But over time, I realized I was leaving opportunities on the table. Not everyone was on Instagram, and my ideal clients were scattered across multiple platforms.

Expanding to new platforms felt overwhelming at first, but I took it step by step. I started by sharing my Instagram posts on Facebook. Then, I began writing LinkedIn articles based on the topics I was already discussing in videos. Finally, I ventured into TikTok, where I discovered a whole new audience that loved short, fun, and relatable clips.

Each platform has its own strengths, and it's worth taking the time to learn what works best on each one. On Facebook, I focus on community-driven content and live videos. On LinkedIn, I share professional insights and success stories. And on TikTok, I embrace trends while keeping them authentic to my brand.

The result? A well-rounded presence that reaches different audiences in different ways. You don't have to master every platform overnight. Start with one or two, get comfortable, and then slowly expand as you go.

Collaborate to Amplify

Collaboration has been one of the most rewarding ways to scale my presence. Whether it's partnering with a local business, hosting a joint event, or teaming up with another professional, collaborations allow you to reach new audiences and create mutually beneficial relationships.

One of my favorite collaborations was with a local boutique that had just opened in town. I approached the owner with an idea: a "Shop & Stage" event where we'd showcase her decor items in one of my listings. She loved the concept, and together, we created an event that blended shopping, home staging, and real estate tours. It brought in a mix of her customers and my clients, and the exposure benefited both of us in ways we couldn't have achieved alone.

Collaborations aren't just about exposure—they're about building relationships that amplify your reach and your impact.

Scaling with Intention

Scaling your presence doesn't mean spreading yourself thin or trying to be everything to everyone. It means being intentional, thinking strategically, and focusing on actions that create the biggest ripple effect.

When you embrace video, build a content ecosystem, expand your platform strategy, and collaborate with others, you create a presence that feels authentic, impactful, and scalable. Most importantly, you create connections that last.

The magic of scaling isn't just about growing your audience—it's about deepening your impact. And in real estate, that impact is what sets you apart.

NINE

Converting Followers into Clients

There was a time when social media felt like a mystery to me. I'd post a photo of a new listing or share a quick market update and wonder: *Is anyone even seeing this?* But everything shifted the day I received a DM that read, *"Hey, Randi, I've been following you for a while and love the way you explain things. My husband and I are thinking about buying a home—can we talk?"*

That message wasn't just a fluke. It was the result of months of intentional effort—posting content that educated, inspired, and connected with my audience. It wasn't about fancy algorithms or viral moments. It was about showing up consistently and creating content that felt real.

The truth is, social media isn't magic, and followers don't just turn into clients overnight. It's about the trust you build, the value you provide, and the relationships you nurture along the way.

Building Connections That Count

One of the biggest misconceptions about social media is that success is measured by follower count. Sure, a large audience can open doors, but what truly matters is the quality of your connections. I've worked with agents who had tens of thousands of followers but struggled to convert them into clients. Why? Because their audience didn't feel a real connection to them.

Think about it: would you trust someone you don't feel connected to with one of the biggest financial decisions of your life? Probably not. That's why the key to converting followers isn't about flashy posts or high production value—it's about building trust, one interaction at a time.

I once posted a simple video explaining the difference between being "under contract" and "pending." It wasn't flashy or groundbreaking, but it was something my audience wanted to know. A few days later, someone messaged me saying, *"I never knew that—thanks for breaking it down! We've been thinking about selling our home, and I'd love to chat with you about the process."*

That moment reinforced what I've come to understand: people don't care about how much you know until they feel like you care about helping them.

The Power of Engagement

When I think about converting followers into clients, engagement is where it all begins. It's not just about responding to comments or liking posts—it's about starting conversations and showing people that you see and value them.

I'll never forget a comment on one of my market update posts. A woman wrote, *"I wish we'd known this before selling our last house. The process was so overwhelming!"* Instead of just replying with, *"Thanks for your comment!"* I wrote back, *"I'm so sorry to hear that. The market can defi-*

nitely feel overwhelming, but I'd love to help if you ever decide to sell again. Let me know if you'd like to chat—I'm here for you!"

That one thoughtful response turned into a DM, which led to a conversation and, eventually, a listing. Engagement isn't just about checking a box—it's about building a bridge between being visible and being approachable.

It's easy to treat engagement like a chore, but the truth is, it's one of the most powerful tools you have. Every comment, every message, and every interaction is an opportunity to show your audience that you're not just a realtor—you're someone who genuinely cares.

Telling Stories That Resonate

People don't remember facts—they remember stories. That's why storytelling is one of the most effective ways to showcase your expertise without feeling like you're "selling."

I once worked with a young couple buying their first home. They were nervous, overwhelmed, and had no idea where to start. I walked them through every step of the process, from securing financing to negotiating their offer. After closing day, I shared their story (with their permission) on social media.

The post wasn't about me—it was about them. I wrote about their journey, the challenges they faced, and the joy of seeing them unlock the door to their dream home. People responded to that post in ways they never had with a generic listing photo. They saw themselves in that couple's story, and it made them feel like I could help them, too.

Stories humanize your brand and build emotional connections. They're not just a way to highlight your successes—they're a way to show your audience that you understand their struggles and know how to help.

The Subtle Art of the Call-to-Action (CTA)

For a long time, I avoided including calls-to-action in my posts. I worried it would come off as pushy or salesy. But then I realized something: a CTA isn't about pressuring people—it's about inviting them to take the next step.

One of my most effective CTAs was in a Reel where I shared tips for preparing a home for sale. At the end, I simply said, *"If you're thinking about selling, send me a message—I'd love to help you get your home market-ready."* That one sentence turned into three new leads in a single day.

The key to a great CTA is to make it natural and actionable. Instead of *"Hire me!"* try something like, *"Send me a message if you'd like to learn more,"* or *"Let's chat about how I can help you."* It's not about creating urgency—it's about creating clarity.

From Followers to Lifelong Relationships

The relationship doesn't end when the transaction does. One of the biggest mistakes agents make is treating clients like one-and-done deals. The real magic happens when you nurture those relationships long after the papers are signed.

For me, this looks like sending handwritten notes after closings, celebrating anniversaries of move-in dates, and staying in touch with small gestures that show I care. I've had clients refer me to friends and family not because I asked, but because they felt valued throughout—and beyond—the process.

One family I worked with told me, *"You're the first realtor who made us feel like more than a transaction. We'll never forget how you made this process so special for us."* That's the kind of loyalty that turns followers into lifelong advocates.

The Long Game of Social Media

Social media isn't a quick fix—it's a long game. Some followers might reach out after weeks; others might take years. But the key is to keep showing up. Every post, every story, every interaction is planting a seed. Some will grow quickly, and others will take time, but when you focus on building trust, the results will come.

Social media isn't just about converting followers—it's about creating connections that last. It's about being the person they think of when they're ready to buy or sell. And when you approach it with patience, authenticity, and a genuine desire to serve, the conversions happen naturally.

TEN

Turning Clients into Advocates

I'll never forget the day I received a text from a past client that said, *"Hey, Randi, I just gave your name to my coworker who's thinking about selling their home. I told her you're the absolute best."* That message felt like a win—not just because it might lead to a new client, but because it proved I had done more than close a deal. I had built a relationship so meaningful that someone was willing to vouch for me to their inner circle.

In real estate, the transaction isn't the finale—it's the opening act. The true magic begins after the keys are handed over. Your clients are more than just buyers and sellers—they are your greatest advocates. A happy client will share your name with friends, family, and coworkers, but only if you've created an experience that's worth sharing.

The Client Experience: More Than a Transaction

Think back to the last time you had exceptional customer service. Maybe it was a server who remembered your name and your favorite order or a boutique owner who wrapped your purchase like it was a gift just for you. Those moments stand out because they made you feel valued, and they probably made you tell others about it.

In real estate, creating that kind of experience is what sets you apart. For me, it always starts with listening—not just to what my clients are saying, but to what they aren't saying. When a young family told me they needed "a little more space," I asked them to describe their weekends. They painted a picture of backyard barbecues, soccer games, and late-night s'mores by a firepit. That image became my focus, and we didn't stop searching until we found a home that fit their vision perfectly.

A month after they moved in, I sent them a text: *"How's that backyard working out for the soccer games?"* They replied with a photo of their kids kicking a ball and wrote, *"Best decision we ever made. Thank you for making it happen."*

That's the kind of experience people remember. It's not just about the sale—it's about making them feel seen, heard, and cared for.

Staying Connected: The Key to Longevity

One of the biggest mistakes realtors make is treating clients like one-and-done transactions. The reality is that your past clients are your most valuable marketing asset—if you nurture the relationship.

For me, staying connected looks like small, meaningful gestures. I send handwritten notes, not just after a closing, but on special anniversaries or milestones. A simple message like, *"Can you believe it's been a year since you moved into your home? I hope it's been everything you dreamed of!"* can reignite that connection and keep you top of mind.

Social media is another way I stay in touch. If I see a past client post about a child's graduation or a family vacation, I take a moment to comment or send a quick message. It's not about selling—it's about showing that I still care about their lives, even after the deal is done.

One of my favorite ways to connect is by hosting small client appreciation events. Whether it's a picnic in the park or a holiday open house, these gatherings create opportunities to reconnect in person, thank them for their trust, and build community among my clients.

Referrals: The Lifeblood of Real Estate

Referrals don't just happen—they're earned. They come from delivering an experience so positive that your clients can't help but tell others about you.

I remember working with a couple who, over the course of a year, referred me to three of their friends. When I asked them what inspired their enthusiasm, they said, *"You didn't just sell us a house—you made us feel like family."* That feedback stuck with me because it reinforced what I've always believed: referrals are about emotional connections, not just professional competence.

To encourage referrals, I make it easy for clients to share my name. After a transaction, I'll say something like, *"If you know anyone who's thinking about buying or selling, I'd be honored if you passed my name along."* It's a simple, direct ask, and it plants the seed for future referrals.

I also like to show appreciation for referrals. If someone sends a client my way, I'll send them a handwritten thank-you note or a small gift, like a coffee shop gift card. It's not about the gift itself—it's about acknowledging their trust in me.

Celebrating Your Clients' Wins

People love to feel celebrated, especially during life-changing moments like buying their first home or upgrading to their dream property. Celebrating your clients isn't just a nice gesture—it's a way to solidify the bond and keep the relationship strong.

One family I worked with had just purchased a home with a huge backyard, perfect for their kids. To celebrate, I surprised them with a basket filled with outdoor games and a personalized note that said,

"Here's to endless soccer games and backyard fun!" They were thrilled, and it made their move-in experience that much more special.

But celebrating doesn't stop after the sale. I make a point to send anniversary messages like, *"Happy 2nd Home-iversary! I hope your house is still full of joy and memories!"* These small, thoughtful gestures show that I'm invested in their happiness for the long haul.

Making It Easy to Advocate

Sometimes, clients want to recommend you but don't know how. That's why it's important to give them tools to make it easy.

I provide every client with a handful of business cards and let them know they're welcome to share my contact information with anyone who might need it. I also encourage them to leave reviews on platforms like Google or Zillow. A simple request like, *"If you enjoyed working with me, I'd love it if you left a review—it really helps me connect with future clients!"* can go a long way.

One initiative I've loved is creating a referral perks program. Whenever someone refers a client to me, I send them a small thank-you gift, like a gift card or a personalized note. It's a way to show appreciation and keep referrals flowing.

Turning Transactions into Lifelong Connections

Here's the secret to turning clients into advocates: it's not about what you do during the transaction—it's about how you show up after. When you treat every client as the start of a lifelong relationship, you create a network of people who not only trust you but are excited to share your name.

It's not about grand gestures or expensive gifts. It's about being genuine, thoughtful, and consistent. The little things—a handwritten note, a thoughtful follow-up, or a small celebration—are what make people feel valued. And when they feel valued, they'll become your biggest advocates.

The effort you invest in your clients today will pay off in loyalty, referrals, and advocacy for years to come. That's the real magic of turning clients into advocates: it's not just about growing your business—it's about building lasting relationships that make every transaction meaningful.

ELEVEN

Mastering Your Local Market

When I started in real estate, I thought success came from knowing the basics—home prices, average days on the market, and how to write a competitive offer. But I quickly learned that numbers alone wouldn't set me apart. Mastering your market isn't about memorizing statistics; it's about understanding the heartbeat of the community, the people who live there, and what truly makes a place feel like home.

This realization hit me during a showing when a couple asked, *"What's the vibe here? Are there young families? What's the traffic like on weekends?"* I froze. I had no idea. I'd been so focused on learning the technical side of real estate that I'd neglected the human side. I left that showing feeling disappointed in myself, but it was also a turning point. From that moment on, I decided I wasn't just going to sell houses—I was going to sell a lifestyle.

Learning the Soul of Your Market

Every town, neighborhood, or city has its own unique personality. Some places exude energy, with buzzing nightlife and trendy cafes. Others feel like a retreat, where quiet streets and sprawling parks make it the perfect escape. Truly mastering your market means understanding these nuances and helping your clients find the one that fits their lives.

I once worked with a couple who were relocating from out of state. They wanted a peaceful neighborhood but also hoped to meet other young families with kids. Instead of jumping straight into showing them houses, I spent time learning about what mattered to them—morning walks with their toddler, a sense of community, and proximity to good schools. I showed them three neighborhoods that matched their lifestyle, taking time to walk with them through local parks and even stopping by a weekend farmers' market so they could see the community in action.

One month after moving in, they sent me a photo of their daughter playing with neighborhood kids in the cul-de-sac and wrote, *"We feel like we've found our forever home. Thank you for helping us get here."*

Understanding the soul of your market isn't just about facts—it's about people. It's about knowing what makes a community special and helping your clients find where they'll feel most at home.

Your Market Is Your Story

Every market tells a story, and as a realtor, you have the privilege of being its storyteller. The local landmarks, traditions, and quirks all play a role in shaping the narrative. When you can bring that story to life for your clients, you're not just selling houses—you're selling a vision of what life could look like.

One of the gems in my market is a historic downtown district, full of charm and character. Whenever a client mentions wanting a "unique" home, I take them there. I'll tell them about the mom-and-pop ice cream shop where generations of locals have celebrated milestones or the annual fall festival that brings everyone together.

I once had a client deciding between two homes. Both were beautiful, but one was near the downtown area, and the other wasn't. When I shared stories of the community—the quirky traditions, the sense of belonging, and even the way neighbors band together to support small businesses—her decision became clear. She said, *"This is the kind of place I've always dreamed of living in."*

Your market's story isn't just a selling point—it's a bridge that helps clients imagine their lives there.

Building Relationships with Local Leaders

When I started in real estate, I underestimated the power of connections. But over time, I learned that relationships with local leaders—like school principals, business owners, and city officials—are invaluable. These people are the gatekeepers of knowledge, and their insights can make all the difference when guiding your clients.

For example, I worked with a family whose top priority was finding a home in a great school district. Instead of simply pointing them to the district's website, I connected them with the principal of a local elementary school. The principal answered their questions, reassured them about their concerns, and shared what made the school special. That conversation sealed the deal for my clients, and it deepened my relationship with the school leader.

Beyond helping clients, these relationships make you a trusted resource in your community. When a new restaurant opens, or a park gets renovated, you'll be one of the first to know—information that adds immense value to your clients.

Turning Challenges into Opportunities

Every market has its challenges. Maybe it's low inventory, soaring prices, or stiff competition. These hurdles might seem discouraging, but they're actually opportunities to stand out by thinking creatively and staying resourceful.

I once worked with a client who was determined to buy in a neighborhood where homes were selling within hours of being listed. Every time we found something she loved, it was already under contract by the next day. Instead of letting her get discouraged, I switched tactics. I started reaching out to homeowners directly—sending handwritten letters, making phone calls, and even knocking on doors to ask if they'd consider selling.

It took persistence, but eventually, I found a homeowner willing to sell to my client. The house never even hit the market, and it ended up being the perfect match.

That experience taught me that challenges are often opportunities in disguise. When you approach them with creativity and determination, you don't just solve problems—you earn your clients' trust for life.

Becoming Synonymous with Your Market

When people think of your market, they should think of you. That kind of recognition doesn't happen overnight—it's the result of consistently showing up, adding value, and positioning yourself as a champion for your community.

For me, this meant getting involved in local events, partnering with small businesses, and creating content that celebrated the unique aspects of my market. One of my favorite projects was hosting a virtual "Best of [Town]" series, where I highlighted everything from the best coffee shops to hidden hiking trails. The series was a hit—not just with my clients, but with the local businesses I featured.

Another way I've made myself synonymous with my market is by sharing local stories on social media. Whether it's spotlighting a new restaurant or posting photos from a community festival, these small efforts help me stay top of mind while showing my love for the place I call home.

Mastering Your Market: A Lifelong Journey

Mastering your local market isn't a one-and-done task—it's an ongoing journey. It's about staying curious, getting involved, and building relationships that help you serve your clients better.

When you understand not just the stats but the soul of your market, you become more than a realtor—you become a guide, a resource, and a trusted advocate. You're the person people turn to when they want more than square footage and sales prices. They come to you for insight, connection, and the promise of finding a place that truly feels like home.

TWELVE

Sustaining Success Through Adaptability and Growth

In real estate, the only constant is change. Markets shift, trends evolve, and what worked last year might not work tomorrow. I've learned that success isn't about avoiding challenges—it's about how you respond to them. The moments that shaped my career the most weren't the easy ones—they were the times I was forced to adapt, innovate, and push beyond my comfort zone.

I still remember the first major shift I faced in the market. It was a slow season, and leads were drying up. Panic started to creep in, but I decided to look at it differently. Instead of focusing on what wasn't working, I saw it as an opportunity to learn. I dove into digital marketing, experimenting with strategies I'd never tried before. I took online courses, revamped my social media presence, and committed to mastering new skills. By the time the market picked up again, I wasn't just surviving—I was thriving.

Success in real estate isn't about coasting through the good times. It's about weathering the storms, learning from the setbacks, and coming out stronger on the other side.

Embrace the Power of Reinvention

One of the biggest lessons I've learned is that success doesn't come from staying the same—it comes from staying relevant. Reinvention isn't about abandoning who you are or what you've built. It's about growing, evolving, and finding new ways to bring value to your clients and your business.

For me, one of the most pivotal reinventions was expanding into luxury real estate. I'll be honest—at first, I wasn't sure I could compete in that space. I doubted whether I had the knowledge, connections, or confidence to break into a market where expectations are sky-high. But instead of letting fear hold me back, I leaned in. I took classes, networked with agents who were already thriving in luxury sales, and studied what made high-end clients tick.

The transition wasn't easy, but it was worth it. Not only did it open up a new revenue stream, but it also forced me to elevate every part of my business—from my marketing to my client interactions. Reinvention doesn't have to mean starting over. Sometimes, it's as simple as refining what you're already doing or exploring a niche that aligns with your strengths.

Learn to Love the Pivot

In real estate, things rarely go exactly as planned. Deals fall through, markets shift, and strategies that used to work suddenly don't. Learning to pivot isn't just a skill—it's a mindset.

I'll never forget an open house I planned early in my career. I'd spent weeks preparing—advertising the event, staging the home, and making sure every detail was perfect. But on the day of the open house, the weather turned nasty, and most of the RSVPs canceled. The few people who did show up seemed more interested in the free snacks than the property.

At first, I felt defeated. But then I asked myself, *What can I do differently next time?* That's when I decided to experiment with virtual open houses. I started creating high-quality video tours that highlighted each home's best features, allowing potential buyers to view properties from the comfort of their own homes.

The shift wasn't just a workaround—it became a powerful new tool in my business. Virtual tours expanded my reach, attracted more serious buyers, and helped me stand out in a crowded market. Pivoting isn't about abandoning your plans—it's about finding new opportunities when the old ones don't pan out.

Invest in Continuous Learning

One of the most important lessons I've learned is that you're never "done" learning. The moment you think you've mastered everything is the moment the industry will prove you wrong. The most successful agents I know are the ones who invest in their growth, whether it's through books, courses, or learning from their peers.

Early in my career, I attended a workshop on digital marketing. At the time, I barely knew how to use social media, let alone leverage it to grow my business. But that workshop transformed the way I connected with clients. I learned how to create content that resonated, engage with my audience authentically, and build a brand that stood out online.

Now, I make it a priority to set aside time for personal and professional development. Whether it's listening to podcasts, attending industry events, or learning about emerging technologies, I'm always looking for ways to stay ahead of the curve.

Celebrate Your Growth

Real estate can feel like a constant hustle, and it's easy to get so focused on what's next that you forget to celebrate how far you've come. But taking time to acknowledge your growth isn't just rewarding—it's necessary.

Every New Year's Eve, I have a tradition of reflecting on the past year. I think about the deals I've closed, the clients I've helped, and the challenges I've overcome. But I don't just celebrate the numbers —I celebrate the impact I've made. I think about the family who found their dream home, the first-time buyers who felt supported every step of the way, and the personal milestones I've reached.

Celebrating your wins, big and small, keep you motivated. It reminds you of what's possible and gives you the energy to keep striving for more.

Adaptability Is Your Superpower

If there's one thing I've learned, it's that adaptability is the most important skill you can have in real estate. Markets will change. Challenges will come. But if you can adapt, you can thrive in any environment.

Every time I've faced a challenge, I've come out stronger because I chose to embrace it. I didn't just survive slow seasons—I used them to learn new skills. I didn't just weather market shifts—I found ways to pivot and create opportunities.

Adaptability isn't just about reacting to change—it's about welcoming it. It's about seeing every obstacle as a chance to grow and every setback as a setup for something greater.

Sustaining Success Through Growth

Sustaining success in real estate isn't about avoiding challenges—it's about learning from them. It's about reinventing yourself when necessary, pivoting when plans go awry, and committing to lifelong learning.

The journey won't always be smooth, but that's what makes it worthwhile. Every time you adapt, every time you grow, you prove to yourself that you're capable of more than you ever thought possible.

Success isn't just about what you achieve—it's about who you become along the way. So embrace the changes, celebrate your wins, and keep moving forward. The best is always yet to come.

THIRTEEN

Leveraging Technology to Elevate Your Business

In today's world, technology isn't just an optional add-on—it's the engine that drives a successful real estate business. From automating tedious tasks to connecting with clients across the globe, the right tools can transform how you work. But let me tell you: I didn't always see it that way.

When I first started incorporating technology into my workflow, I was hesitant. I'm a people person, and I worried that apps and platforms would make my business feel cold and impersonal. But as I dug deeper, I realized that technology doesn't replace relationships—it enhances them. It frees up time, expands your reach, and helps you focus on what really matters: serving your clients and connecting with people.

The real magic of technology is how it amplifies your ability to show up authentically while streamlining the behind-the-scenes work that keeps your business running smoothly.

Creating a Seamless Client Experience

Technology's biggest superpower? It makes the client experience smoother, simpler, and more memorable. From the moment someone reaches out to you to the day they hold the keys to their new home, tech tools can help you stay on top of every detail.

For me, a game-changer has been my customer relationship management (CRM) software. It's like having a digital assistant who never forgets anything. I can track conversations, schedule reminders, and even note personal details that might come in handy later.

One time, a client casually mentioned they'd be celebrating their anniversary the weekend before their move. I added it to their file in my CRM, and two months later, I sent them a congratulatory message. That small, thoughtful touch not only surprised them but also deepened our connection. They told me later, *"You're not just a realtor—you're someone who truly listens."*

Streamlining processes with tools like CRMs isn't about replacing personal touches—it's about enabling them. You're not bogged down by the logistics, so you can focus on the moments that matter.

Showcasing Listings Like Never Before

Gone are the days of static photos and print ads being enough to sell a home. Today's buyers expect immersive, interactive experiences that help them envision their future before they even step inside. That's where technology steps in.

I remember working with a family relocating from another state. They couldn't tour homes in person, so I created a virtual walk-through of a property, pointing out features and describing the neighborhood as if we were walking through it together. I even included shots of the local park and nearby restaurants. By the end of the video, they said, *"It feels like we've already been there."*

Tools like virtual tours, drone photography, and 3D staging bring listings to life. They let clients imagine the possibilities, even from miles away. And in today's competitive market, these tools don't just elevate your listings—they elevate your reputation.

Automating the Mundane

In real estate, there's no shortage of repetitive tasks. Scheduling showings, managing paperwork, and sending follow-up emails can eat up hours of your day. That's where automation becomes your best friend.

The first time I used an automated email sequence, I was blown away. A lead had signed up for my newsletter, and within days, they were receiving a series of personalized emails with tips for first-time buyers. By the time we spoke on the phone, they already trusted me as an expert. *"Your emails answered all my questions before I even asked them,"* they said.

Automation doesn't just save time—it makes you look like you're everywhere, all at once. Tools like e-signature platforms, scheduling apps, and automated follow-ups let you work smarter while maintaining a professional, polished image.

Reaching Clients Where They Are

Technology has completely reshaped how we connect with potential clients. Social media, email campaigns, and search engine marketing give you the power to meet people where they're already spending their time.

One of my most memorable moments came from a 30-second TikTok I posted about mistakes first-time buyers make. It was quick, casual, and packed with value. Within hours, my inbox was full of messages from viewers saying, *"I had no idea! Can you help me avoid these mistakes?"* That single post turned into three new clients in just one week.

But it's not just about creating content—it's about understanding what works. By analyzing engagement metrics, I've been able to tailor my posts to topics my audience cares about, from market updates to home staging tips. The result? More meaningful connections and a steady stream of leads.

Balancing Tech with a Personal Touch

As powerful as technology is, it's not a substitute for human connection. No app can replace the warmth of a phone call or the sincerity of a handwritten note. That's why I see tech as a tool, not the foundation of my business.

For every virtual tour I create, there's a follow-up call to answer questions. For every automated email I send, there's a handwritten thank-you note after the deal closes. It's this balance—combining efficiency with authenticity—that keeps my business grounded in what matters most: people.

I once helped a couple purchase their first home. After closing, I sent them an automated email with tips for settling in, but I also stopped by their house a week later with a basket of housewarming gifts. The combination of high-tech and high-touch left them saying, *"You've thought of everything."*

Why Technology Matters

Leveraging technology isn't about being the most tech-savvy realtor in the game—it's about using the tools available to enhance your strengths. It's about working smarter so you can spend more time connecting with people, understanding their needs, and delivering exceptional service.

With the right balance of tools and personal touches, you can create a business that feels modern yet deeply human. Technology isn't replacing relationships—it's making them stronger.

Sustaining Success Through Innovation

The real estate industry is always evolving, and staying ahead means embracing the tools that make your job easier, your service better, and your business more visible. From automating mundane tasks to creating unforgettable listing experiences, technology lets you do more of what you love while giving your clients an experience they'll never forget.

Adapt, innovate, and always keep your clients at the heart of what you do. Because at the end of the day, technology isn't the star—you are.

FOURTEEN

Building a Team and Expanding Your Reach

When I started my real estate career, I was a one-woman show. I took pride in doing it all—answering calls, showing homes, drafting contracts, scheduling appointments, and even handling my marketing. I believed that if I worked hard enough, I could manage everything myself. And for a while, I did.

But as my business grew, so did the demands on my time and energy. I'll never forget one particularly chaotic week. I was juggling multiple clients, rushing from back-to-back showings, trying to organize my kids' activities, and staying up late to finish paperwork. One night, after tucking my kids into bed, I sat at my desk, completely exhausted. My to-do list seemed endless, and I realized something had to give.

That's when it hit me: I didn't need to do it all. In fact, trying to do it all was holding me back. If I wanted to serve my clients at the highest level and still have time for my family, I needed help.

The Decision to Build a Team

Deciding to build a team wasn't easy. I wrestled with doubts: *Am I ready? Can I afford it? Will clients still want to work with me if I'm not doing everything myself?* But as my workload grew, it became clear that staying in "solo mode" was limiting my potential.

My first step was hiring an assistant to handle administrative tasks like scheduling, managing emails, and organizing paperwork. It was a small step, but it made an enormous difference. Suddenly, I had breathing room. I could focus on what I did best—building relationships, negotiating deals, and growing my brand.

Once I saw how much value my assistant added, I started to think bigger. I brought on a buyer's agent to handle showings and a marketing coordinator to elevate my listings. Each new team member brought fresh ideas and unique strengths, and together, we created a business that could accomplish far more than I ever could on my own.

Building a team wasn't just about delegating tasks—it was about creating a system that allowed me to grow sustainably and serve my clients even better.

Finding the Right People

When I started building my team, I knew one thing for sure: I didn't just want employees—I wanted partners who shared my vision and values. Skills can be taught, but passion and alignment are non-negotiable.

I'll never forget interviewing my first buyer's agent. She was new to real estate but had a background in customer service and a natural ability to connect with people. She told me, *"I want to help people find homes, not just houses."* That one sentence told me everything I needed to know. She cared about the work, the clients, and the experience, and I knew she'd be a great fit.

Over time, I've learned that hiring the right people isn't just about their resume—it's about their attitude, work ethic, and willingness to grow. I look for team members who are driven, eager to learn, and genuinely care about making a difference.

Creating a Culture of Collaboration

A great team isn't just a collection of individuals—it's a cohesive unit working toward a shared goal. To build that kind of synergy, I've made it a priority to foster a culture of collaboration, trust, and mutual respect.

For me, this starts with communication. We hold regular team meetings where we celebrate wins, tackle challenges, and brainstorm ideas. I make sure every team member feels valued and empowered to take ownership of their role.

One of my proudest moments came when my marketing coordinator pitched an idea for a social media campaign that ended up doubling our engagement. Watching her take the initiative and seeing her creativity pay off reminded me why building a collaborative team is so powerful.

When your team feels supported and empowered, they don't just do their job—they exceed expectations.

Scaling Without Losing Your Touch

One of my biggest fears about building a team was losing the personal touch that set my business apart. I worried that clients might feel disconnected if I wasn't the one handling every detail. But I quickly realized that scaling isn't about stepping back—it's about stepping up in new ways.

By delegating administrative and operational tasks, I could focus more on the parts of the business that truly needed my attention—like building relationships, creating content, and ensuring my clients had an exceptional experience. I made it a point to stay involved in key moments, like initial consultations and closing celebrations, while trusting my team to handle the rest.

One client told me, *"Your team is incredible. It feels like everyone is working together to make this process seamless."* That's exactly the feedback I hoped for. It's not about me doing everything—it's about creating a system where every client feels supported and valued.

Expanding Your Reach

Building a team isn't just about doing more—it's about reaching more people. With the right team in place, I've been able to take on opportunities I never thought possible.

One of the most fulfilling parts of expanding my reach has been mentoring new agents. Watching them grow, succeed, and bring fresh ideas to the table has been one of the most rewarding aspects of my career. It's not just about growing my business—it's about building a legacy.

I've also been able to explore new niches, like luxury real estate and relocation services. By leveraging my team's diverse skills and expertise, I've expanded into markets and opportunities that I couldn't have tackled alone.

When you build a team, you're not just multiplying your capacity—you're multiplying your impact.

The Rewards of Leadership

Looking back, building a team has been one of the most challenging and rewarding decisions of my career. It's taught me the value of trust, the power of collaboration, and the importance of leadership.

There's something incredibly fulfilling about seeing your team thrive, your clients happy, and your business grow. I've gone from feeling overwhelmed and overworked to feeling empowered and energized. And I've built a business that's not just successful—it's sustainable.

Leadership isn't just about delegating tasks—it's about empowering others to succeed. When your team grows, your business grows, and together, you can achieve more than you ever could alone.

Building Your Legacy

Building a team is more than a business strategy—it's a way to create a lasting impact. It's about mentoring others, expanding your reach, and creating a business that reflects your values.

As I look to the future, I'm excited to see how my team will continue to grow and evolve. Because at the end of the day, success isn't just about what you achieve—it's about the legacy you leave behind.

FIFTEEN

Overcoming Challenges in Real Estate

Real estate is often romanticized as the perfect career: flexible hours, the thrill of closing deals, and endless opportunities to build wealth. But the reality is more complex. For every success story, there's a setback. For every "Congratulations, you're under contract!" there's a deal that falls apart or a client who decides to work with someone else.

Challenges in real estate aren't the exception—they're the norm. But they're also where the most growth happens. The moments that test your patience, resilience, and creativity are the same ones that help you evolve into a stronger, more confident agent.

I've faced my fair share of these moments. From market crashes to difficult clients, from rejection to balancing work and life, the road hasn't been easy. But each challenge has taught me something invaluable—not just about real estate, but about myself.

Lesson 1: You Can't Control the Market

When I started in real estate, I believed hard work and determination were enough to guarantee success. But it didn't take long to learn that the market plays its own game. It doesn't care about your plans, your goals, or how many hours you're willing to put in.

I'll never forget my first market downturn. It felt like the world had stopped. Listings lingered on the market, buyers disappeared, and the deals I had been counting on evaporated overnight. I spent hours stressing, asking myself, *What now? How do I make this work?*

Instead of throwing in the towel, I pivoted. I shifted my focus to rentals, a niche I hadn't previously considered. Helping landlords find tenants and families secure short-term housing wasn't glamorous, but it kept me afloat. And it taught me a critical lesson: survival in this business isn't about resisting the market—it's about adapting to it.

The market will always change. Some seasons will bring prosperity, while others will test your limits. Your job isn't to fight those changes but to find opportunities within them.

Lesson 2: Difficult Clients Are Your Best Teachers

Every realtor has a story about *that client*. The one who tests your patience and pushes you to your limits. For me, it was a couple who couldn't agree on anything. Every showing turned into a debate, with one loving the layout and the other fixating on the flaws. I felt more like a referee than a realtor.

One day, after yet another round of disagreements, I decided to try something different. I sat them down and said, "Let's forget about specifics for a moment. Tell me what 'home' means to you—what it feels like, what it looks like, what it gives you." That conversation changed everything. Instead of focusing on their differences, they started dreaming together.

In the end, we found a home that they both adored. That experience wasn't just a win for them—it was a turning point for me. It taught me the power of empathy, active listening, and patience. Difficult clients aren't obstacles; they're opportunities to grow.

Lesson 3: Rejection Is Part of the Process

Rejection is one of the hardest parts of real estate. Whether it's losing a listing to another agent or having a deal fall through at the last minute, rejection can feel deeply personal.

Early in my career, I lost a listing I'd worked tirelessly to secure. The sellers chose another agent who, they said, had "more experience." I was crushed. But instead of dwelling on it, I reached out to ask what had influenced their decision. Their feedback was simple but powerful: the other agent had a stronger marketing plan.

That rejection was a wake-up call. I invested in training, upgraded my tools, and developed a marketing strategy that set me apart. The next time I pitched myself to a client, I walked in with confidence—and won the listing.

Rejection isn't the end of the road. It's a detour, guiding you toward areas where you can grow and improve. The key is to see every "no" as an opportunity to learn and come back stronger.

Lesson 4: Balancing Real Estate and Real Life

Real estate doesn't come with a clock-in, clock-out schedule. There are late-night calls, weekend showings, and endless emails. For me, balancing work and family has been one of the toughest challenges.

There was one week that stands out. My daughter had a school play, my son had a baseball tournament, and I had three closings on the horizon. I was stretched so thin that I felt like I was failing at everything. That week, I made a decision: I was going to set boundaries.

Now, I treat family commitments like non-negotiable appointments. If my son has a game, it goes on the calendar. If a client asks for a showing during that time, I offer an alternative. Setting boundaries hasn't just improved my personal life—it's made me a better agent. When I show up for clients, I'm fully present because I've already prioritized what matters most.

Work-life balance in real estate is a constant juggle, but it's possible when you prioritize and plan.

Lesson 5: Building Confidence Through Failure

Failure is inevitable in real estate. There will be listings you can't sell, deals that fall apart, and strategies that flop. But failure isn't a verdict—it's a teacher.

One of my hardest lessons came with a luxury listing I just couldn't move. It was a beautiful property, but I struggled to find the right buyer. After months of effort, the sellers decided to go with another agent. I felt defeated, but instead of giving up, I asked myself: *What can I learn from this?*

I studied how other agents marketed high-end properties, took a course on luxury real estate, and adjusted my approach. The next time I landed a luxury listing, I sold it in record time. That failure wasn't a setback—it was a stepping stone.

Every failure is an opportunity to refine your skills, deepen your knowledge, and build the confidence to tackle bigger challenges.

Resilience Is Your Superpower

If there's one lesson real estate has taught me, it's that resilience is the key to success. Challenges will come, but they don't define you. How you respond to them does.

When I look back on my journey, it's the tough moments that stand out—not because they were painful, but because they pushed me to grow. They taught me to adapt, to persevere, and to trust in my ability to navigate whatever comes my way.

Real estate isn't just about selling homes—it's about building relationships, solving problems, and showing up when it counts. And every challenge is an opportunity to prove to yourself—and your clients—that you're up to the task.

The Takeaway

Challenges aren't roadblocks—they're stepping stones. They force you to think creatively, act courageously, and grow into the agent you're meant to be. So the next time you face a tough client, a shifting market, or a moment of doubt, remember this: you're stronger than you think, and every challenge is preparing you for something greater.

SIXTEEN

The Psychology of Selling

Real estate isn't just about contracts, listings, or negotiations. At its core, it's about people—their hopes, dreams, fears, and memories. Every buyer and seller comes to the table with a unique story, shaped by their emotions and aspirations. To succeed in real estate, you need more than market knowledge; you need to understand the human side of every transaction.

When I first started in this business, I focused heavily on facts and figures. I believed that if I presented the right data, the decision would naturally follow. But I quickly realized that buying or selling a home is rarely about numbers—it's about feelings. The way you make someone feel during the process can shape their entire experience and determine whether they trust you, recommend you, and work with you again.

Let's explore the emotional landscape of real estate and how understanding it can elevate your success.

Understanding Buyer Psychology: Emotion Meets Practicality

When buyers step into a home, their decision-making begins with an emotional reaction. It's the flutter of excitement when they imagine their kids playing in the backyard, the comfort of picturing Sunday mornings in a cozy kitchen, or the spark of inspiration when they see a sunlit living room. These emotions often outweigh the logical considerations, at least initially.

I remember working with a young couple, both engineers, who approached their home search like a checklist. They wanted to know the square footage, roof condition, and proximity to work. But when we walked into a charming house with a wraparound porch, their checklist disappeared. They stood quietly, soaking in the space. The wife turned to me and said, "I don't know what it is, but this feels like home."

That moment was pivotal. My role wasn't to let their emotions override practicality—it was to balance the two. While they were enamored with the house, I reminded them to consider the commute, potential repairs, and long-term suitability. In the end, they bought the home, but only after ensuring it fit their practical needs as well.

How to Tap Into Buyer Psychology

- Ask open-ended questions: "How do you imagine spending your weekends here?" or "What's the first thing you'd do after moving in?"
- Pay attention to body language—are they lingering in a certain room, smiling more than usual, or visibly relaxed?
- Guide their emotions with facts, helping them align their excitement with practicality.

Understanding Seller Psychology: The Emotional Goodbye

Selling a home is rarely just a financial decision. It's often an emotional goodbye to a chapter of life. For some, it's the home where they raised their children. For others, it's a place where they overcame challenges or celebrated milestones. Letting go can feel like losing a piece of themselves.

One retired couple I worked with had lived in their home for over 40 years. The husband was eager to downsize, but the wife was hesitant. She kept bringing up memories tied to every corner of the house—Christmas mornings by the fireplace and summer barbecues in the backyard. Each showing felt like an invasion of their personal history.

Rather than rushing her, I listened. I validated her feelings and reframed the sale as an opportunity to pass the home to a new family who would create their own memories. When I presented an offer from a couple with young kids, I shared a note they'd written about their plans to build a treehouse in the yard. It was the turning point. For the first time, the wife smiled and said, "It's time for someone else to love this home."

How to Support Sellers Through the Transition:

- Acknowledge their emotions before diving into logistics.
- Help them see the sale as a positive step forward, not just a loss.
- Use storytelling to connect the buyers' future with the sellers' past.

Building Trust: The Bedrock of Every Transaction

Trust isn't something you can fake—it's built brick by brick through honesty, consistency, and genuine care. In real estate, trust is the difference between a client feeling confident in your advice or questioning your every move.

For me, trust starts with setting clear expectations. If I know a seller's price is unrealistic based on market conditions, I don't sugarcoat it. I say, "I understand why you want to aim high, but here's what the data tells us. Let's discuss how we can position your home to attract the right buyers." They may not love hearing it, but they appreciate my honesty—and that honesty builds trust.

Similarly, when working with buyers, I prioritize transparency. If I notice potential issues during a showing, I point them out. "This home is beautiful, but I'd want to take a closer look at the foundation before moving forward." By putting their interests above the sale, I demonstrate that I'm an advocate, not just a salesperson.

Ways to Build Trust

- Always deliver on your promises, no matter how small.
- Be proactive in addressing concerns, even if it's uncomfortable.
- Show your clients that their goals—not yours—are your top priority.

The Power of Reciprocity: Small Gestures, Big Impact

People naturally want to reciprocate kindness. In real estate, going the extra mile for your clients often inspires them to do the same for you. It's not about manipulation—it's about creating genuine moments of connection.

One time, after helping a family relocate, I gifted them a framed map of their new city with a note saying, "Here's to all the adventures ahead." They were so touched that they referred me to multiple friends and even left a glowing review. That one thoughtful gesture turned into a ripple effect of opportunities.

How to Practice Reciprocity

- Send handwritten thank-you notes after closings.
- Celebrate your clients' milestones, like anniversaries or new additions to their family.
- Surprise them with a small, meaningful gift that reflects their interests.

Balancing Logic and Emotion: The Sweet Spot of Selling

Real estate decisions often sit at the intersection of logic and emotion. Buyers want to feel excited about their new home but also need to feel confident it's a wise investment. Sellers want to honor their emotional ties but also need to make financially sound choices.

Your role as a realtor is to guide your clients through this balancing act. It's not about pushing them in one direction—it's about walking alongside them, providing perspective, and empowering them to make decisions they'll feel good about.

I've found that the most successful transactions happen when clients feel both understood and informed. They trust you to handle the details because you've taken the time to understand their hearts.

Bridging the Gap:

- Use stories and data together: "This home has the charm you love, and it's also in a neighborhood with rising property values."
- Be patient with indecision—it's a natural part of emotional and logical alignment.

Resonating Beyond the Sale

When the paperwork is signed, and the keys are exchanged, your clients won't just remember the deal—they'll remember how you made them feel. Did they feel supported? Heard? Respected? Your ability to understand the psychology behind their decisions will determine the answer.

Real estate isn't just about closing deals—it's about creating experiences. It's about helping people navigate one of the most emotional and significant decisions of their lives with confidence and care.

The Takeaway

Understanding the psychology of selling transforms you from a good realtor into an exceptional one. By recognizing the emotions that drive decisions and balancing them with practical guidance, you create trust, loyalty, and unforgettable experiences. This is the art of real estate—not just selling properties, but serving people.

SEVENTEEN

The Future of Real Estate: Embracing Change and Defining Your Path

Real estate has always been an industry of change. Markets rise and fall, trends come and go, and technology continuously reshapes the landscape. But the changes we've seen in the last decade—particularly over the last few years—have felt more like a seismic shift. For many agents, including me, it's been a whirlwind of adapting to new tools, new expectations, and entirely new ways of connecting with clients.

The future of real estate isn't about surviving these changes; it's about thriving in them. It's about leaning into the opportunities that come with innovation and using them to elevate not just your business but the experience you provide to your clients. For me, that realization wasn't immediate—it was a journey. A journey that began long before I picked up my phone to film my first property video and one that continues to evolve every single day.

Hesitation and the First Steps

When I started in real estate, the idea of using video to market properties felt like a distant concept. Social media itself was still finding its footing, and platforms like Instagram and Facebook were seen as tools for personal use rather than business. I was like many agents at the time—focused on traditional methods. Open houses, direct mail campaigns, and face-to-face networking were my bread and butter. They worked, and I was comfortable with them.

Video, on the other hand, felt intimidating. I wasn't a filmmaker, and I certainly didn't consider myself the kind of person who could be "on camera." It wasn't just about the technology—it was about the vulnerability. Putting yourself out there in such an exposed way felt risky, and at the time, I wasn't sure if the reward would be worth it.

Looking back, I realize that my hesitation was rooted in fear—fear of judgment, fear of failure, and fear of stepping out of my comfort zone. And while those fears didn't disappear overnight, what eventually pushed me forward was necessity. Sometimes, the greatest motivator isn't inspiration—it's survival.

The Catalyst: Navigating a Pandemic

The COVID-19 pandemic was a turning point for all of us. For me, it wasn't just a personal challenge—it was a professional one. Almost overnight, the traditional ways of doing business were gone. Open houses were canceled, in-person meetings were impossible, and the future of the market felt uncertain. I remember sitting in my office one day, staring at a calendar full of crossed-out appointments, wondering what my next move would be.

I had two choices: I could wait for things to return to normal, or I could adapt. Waiting, of course, wasn't really an option. I had a family to support and a business to sustain. So, I took a deep breath, grabbed my phone, and started filming.

The first video I made was far from perfect. It was a walkthrough of a listing, filmed with shaky hands and no script. I simply talked about what I loved about the home and why I thought it would be a great fit for the right buyer. It wasn't polished, but it was real. And to my surprise, people responded.

That first video sparked something in me. I began experimenting with live virtual tours, hosting Facebook Lives where potential buyers could ask questions in real-time. I started sharing more about my day-to-day life—homeschooling my kids, cooking dinner, and even the occasional chaotic moment of trying to balance it all. It wasn't just about showing homes; it was about showing people who I was.

Finding My Voice Through Video

As the months went on, I began to see video not as a tool but as a language—a way to communicate, connect, and build trust. For years, I had relied on face-to-face interactions to build relationships with clients. Now, I was learning how to do that through a screen. And what I discovered was that the authenticity of the video could create a connection that was just as strong, if not stronger.

Video became my way of telling stories. I wasn't just showing properties; I was sharing the lives that could be lived within them. A sunny kitchen wasn't just a feature—it was the place where a family could gather for breakfast on a lazy Sunday morning. A backyard with a pool wasn't just an amenity—it was where summer memories would be made. Through video, I could paint a picture of what a home could mean, not just what it looked like.

This storytelling approach wasn't just effective—it was transformative. Buyers felt like they already knew me before we ever spoke, and sellers saw the effort I was putting into marketing their properties in a fresh and creative way. Video wasn't just a part of my business anymore—it was my business.

A Shift in Perspective

What surprised me most about embracing video wasn't the technical side—it was the personal growth that came with it. In the beginning, I was so focused on the mechanics—what to say, how to angle the camera, what lighting to use—that I didn't realize the real work was happening inside me.

Putting yourself on video is vulnerable. There's no hiding behind a script or an email. People see you—your expressions, your tone, your energy. At first, that vulnerability felt overwhelming. But over time, it became empowering. I learned to trust myself, to let go of perfection, and to show up exactly as I was. And in doing so, I found that people connected with me not in spite of my imperfections but because of them.

Looking Ahead: The Future of Real Estate

As I think about the future of real estate, I feel a sense of excitement and possibility. The industry is changing faster than ever, but with change comes opportunity. Technology will continue to play a massive role, but at its core, real estate will always be about people. It's about listening, understanding, and building relationships that go beyond transactions.

The lessons I've learned over the past few years have given me a vision for what's next. I see a future where agents aren't just salespeople but storytellers and trusted advisors. Where our role isn't just to market homes but to create meaningful connections with the people who live in them. And where the tools we use—whether it's video, social media, or virtual reality—enhance, rather than replace, the human experience.

For me, the future isn't about predicting what's next; it's about being ready to adapt, innovate, and show up with authenticity and heart. It's about staying curious, embracing the unknown, and remembering why we do this work in the first place: to help people find not just houses but homes.

A Final Reflection

If there's one thing I've learned on this journey, it's that the future of real estate isn't something we wait for—it's something we create. Every video I post, every story I share, and every client I connect with is a step toward shaping what's next. And, as I continue to grow and evolve, I know one thing for sure: video will always be at the heart of my business. It's not just a tool—it's my voice, my brand, and my way of making an impact.

The road ahead is full of possibilities, and I can't wait to see where it leads. For me, for my clients, and for the future of real estate.

Bonus Chapter: Coaching with Cardone—Taking Real Estate to the Next Level

When I began my real estate career, my vision was simple: help people find their dream homes while building a thriving business. Back then, I was focused on the day-to-day grind —open houses, cold calls, and client meetings. I didn't realize how much more I could accomplish by stepping into a coaching role, sharing my knowledge, and guiding others. It wasn't until I discovered the power of mentorship and joined Grant Cardone's 10X platform that I understood the ripple effect coaching could create, not just in my life but in the lives of others.

Stepping into the world of coaching wasn't a decision I made lightly. It required me to stretch beyond what I thought I was capable of. Coaching isn't just about imparting knowledge—it's about transformation. It's about helping others see their potential while pushing yourself to grow even further. It's a responsibility, yes, but it's also an extraordinary privilege.

The Leap into Coaching

The idea of becoming a coach can feel daunting. I get it. Leadership brings with it new responsibilities, greater accountability, and a sense of vulnerability. There's this inner voice that whispers, *Who am I to coach others? What if I fail?* I felt all of that. But I also felt something stronger—a deep desire to give back and help others achieve their own version of success.

I didn't set out to be a coach. My journey started with a simple realization: the more I learned, the more I wanted to share. Every time I closed a deal or overcame a challenge, I found myself thinking, *How can I help someone else do this too?* That mindset led me to Grant Cardone's 10X philosophy, a way of thinking that completely transformed my approach to business and life.

The Power of 10X

Before embracing the 10X mindset, I often found myself playing small. I set goals that felt safe and stayed within the boundaries of what I thought I could achieve. But Cardone's teachings challenged me to dream bigger. The 10X philosophy is built around the idea of setting goals so audacious they scare you and then taking massive, focused action to achieve them.

For me, one of those 10X goals was to expand beyond individual transactions and create a legacy. I wanted to build a brand, a team, and a platform that could impact not just my clients but the entire real estate community. It felt overwhelming at first, like trying to climb a mountain with no map. But I started small—one step, one action, one win at a time. That's the beauty of 10X: it's not about perfection. It's about progress.

Transforming Through Action

One of the greatest lessons I've learned through Cardone's coaching is the importance of taking action. In real estate, as in life, it's easy to get stuck in planning mode. We draft strategies, make lists, and analyze every angle, but none of that matters if we don't take the next step.

I'll never forget the first time I applied this principle. I had just completed one of Cardone's training sessions and was fired up about implementing what I'd learned. Instead of overthinking, I picked up the phone and started making calls. By the end of the day, I had booked three new client meetings. It wasn't because I had the perfect pitch or script—it was because I acted. That momentum carried me forward, and I've never looked back.

From Realtor to Coach

Becoming a coach wasn't just about adding a new title to my resume—it was about expanding my impact. As a realtor, I could help individual clients achieve their goals. As a coach, I could empower other realtors to do the same, creating a ripple effect of success that reaches buyers, sellers, and entire communities.

One of the most rewarding parts of coaching is watching others grow. I've worked with agents who started with no confidence, no leads, and no clear direction. Through coaching, I've seen them transform—not just their businesses but their mindsets and lives. There's nothing more fulfilling than watching someone step into their potential.

I remember working with one agent in particular, a woman who had just started in real estate and was struggling to find her footing. She doubted herself, worried about rejection, and felt invisible in a competitive market. Through weekly coaching sessions, we worked on shifting her mindset, refining her personal brand, and building her confidence. Within six months, she had doubled her income and built a thriving client base. Watching her succeed reminded me why I do this work.

The Challenges of Coaching

Coaching isn't always easy. It requires patience, empathy, and a willingness to meet people where they are. Not every agent I've worked with has been ready to embrace change. Some resist the process, clinging to old habits or limiting beliefs. But those moments are opportunities for growth—not just for the person I'm coaching but for me as well.

Coaching is a two-way street. Every person I mentor challenges me to think differently, communicate more effectively, and lead with intention. It's not about having all the answers—it's about being willing to learn alongside your clients.

A Personal Transformation

Stepping into a coaching role has transformed me in ways I never expected. It's pushed me to refine my skills, expand my mindset, and lead with purpose. But more than that, it's deepened my sense of gratitude and fulfillment. Coaching isn't just about helping others—it's about becoming the best version of yourself in the process.

Before I embraced coaching, I often felt like I was running on a hamster wheel—working hard but not necessarily working smart. Cardone's programs taught me to think strategically, dream bigger, and take ownership of my success. Coaching gave me a platform to share those lessons with others, amplifying their impact.

Looking Ahead: The Legacy of Coaching

As I continue this journey, my goal is simple: to help as many people as possible reach their full potential. Coaching isn't about creating carbon copies of yourself—it's about empowering others to find their unique path to success. It's about inspiring confidence, fostering growth, and leaving a lasting impact.

Real estate is an incredible industry, but it can also be challenging. The highs are exhilarating, but the lows can be tough. That's why coaching matters. It's not just about teaching strategies—it's about providing support, encouragement, and perspective. It's about reminding people that they're capable of more than they realize.

Through coaching, I've seen firsthand the power of belief. When you believe in someone—when you show them what's possible—it changes everything. They start to believe in themselves, and that belief fuels action. Action creates results, and results build momentum. It's a cycle of growth that has no limits.

Coaching with Cardone has been one of the most transformative experiences of my life. It's taught me that success isn't just about what you achieve—it's about what you help others achieve. It's about creating a legacy that extends far beyond your own career.

If you're considering stepping into a coaching role or applying coaching principles to your own life, my advice is simple: start where you are. You don't need to have all the answers or a perfect plan. You just need the willingness to take action, learn as you go, and lead with authenticity.

The journey won't always be easy, but it will be worth it. Because when you empower others to succeed, you create a ripple effect of growth, transformation, and impact that can change the world—one person, one goal, and one step at a time.

Your Journey Starts Here

When I look back on my real estate career, it's clear that success wasn't a straight path—it was a winding road filled with challenges, triumphs, and moments of self-discovery. There were times when I doubted myself, questioned my abilities, and wondered if I had what it took to thrive in this industry. But with every setback, I found an opportunity to grow, and with every success, I discovered new ways to push myself further.

Writing this book has been a reflection of that journey. Each chapter represents not just a lesson I've learned, but a piece of the puzzle that brought me to where I am today. And now, it's your turn to take these lessons and make them your own.

The Core Truths of Real Estate and Life

At its core, this book is about more than real estate—it's about personal growth, resilience, and the power of believing in yourself. Whether you're an aspiring realtor, a seasoned professional, or simply someone looking for inspiration, the principles we've explored together can be applied to any area of your life.

1. Your Brand Is Your Foundation

Everything starts with your brand—your unique identity, your values, and the way you show up in the world. Your brand isn't just about marketing—it's about connection. It's what makes people trust you, remember you, and choose you over the competition.

Key Takeaway:

Be authentic. Build a brand that reflects who you are and what you stand for. People will be drawn to your honesty and integrity.

2. Resilience Is Your Superpower

Real estate, like life, is full of ups and downs. Deals fall through, clients walk away, and markets change. But every challenge is an opportunity to learn, adapt, and come back stronger.

Key Takeaway:

Don't fear failure—embrace it. Every setback is a stepping stone to success.

3. The Power of Relationships

At the heart of real estate is one simple truth: it's a people business. Building trust, understanding client psychology, and nurturing long-term relationships are what set great agents apart from good ones.

Key Takeaway:

Focus on relationships, not transactions. When you genuinely care about people, success follows.

4. Mindset Matters

Your mindset shapes your reality. Whether it's embracing the 10X philosophy, staying adaptable, or setting bold goals, your attitude determines your altitude.

Key Takeaway:

Think big, act big, and refuse to settle for anything less than your full potential.

Looking Ahead: The Future Is Yours

The real estate industry is constantly evolving, and the future belongs to those who are willing to embrace change. Whether it's leveraging technology, exploring new markets, or redefining what it means to be a realtor, the possibilities are endless. But staying ahead requires more than just keeping up with trends—it requires a commitment to growth.

As I've navigated the twists and turns of my own career, one thing has remained constant: the importance of adaptability. The agents who thrive in this business aren't the ones who stick to the same old strategies—they're the ones who innovate, pivot, and find new ways to create value for their clients.

A Personal Reflection:

I've learned that success isn't about having all the answers—it's about being willing to ask questions, try new things, and take risks. Some of the greatest opportunities in my career came from moments of uncertainty—moments when I chose to step out of my comfort zone and embrace the unknown.

Your Call to Action

This book isn't just a collection of stories and advice—it's a blueprint for action. But reading it isn't enough. The real transformation happens when you take what you've learned and put it into practice. Here's your challenge:

1. **Set Your Goals:** What do you want to achieve in the next year? The next five years? Write down your goals, and don't be afraid to dream big.
2. **Take Massive Action:** Break your goals into actionable steps, and start taking them today. Remember, small steps lead to big results.
3. **Invest in Yourself:** Whether it's through coaching, education, or self-reflection, commit to your own growth. You are your greatest asset.
4. **Build Your Legacy:** Success isn't just about what you accomplish—it's about the impact you have on others. Focus on creating a life and career that leaves a lasting mark.

The Ripple Effect of Leadership

One of the most rewarding parts of my journey has been stepping into a coaching role. Helping others succeed has shown me that true leadership isn't about being in charge—it's about serving others. Whether you're mentoring a colleague, inspiring a client, or leading by example, your actions have the power to create a ripple effect of growth and empowerment.

A Vision for the Future

I believe that the future of real estate—and of any industry—lies in collaboration, innovation, and shared success. As you move forward, remember that your journey isn't just about you. Every choice you make, every lesson you share, and every action you take has the potential to inspire someone else.

A Personal Thank You

Before we close this chapter, I want to take a moment to thank you. Thank you for investing your time in this book, for believing in your potential, and for taking the first step toward your next level of success. Writing this book has been a labor of love—a way to share my story, my lessons, and my passion with people like you who are ready to make a difference.

I hope you leave these pages feeling inspired, empowered, and equipped to take on whatever challenges and opportunities come your way. Because if there's one thing I know for sure, it's this: you have everything it takes to succeed.

Final Thoughts: It's Your Time

The real estate industry is full of opportunities, but the greatest opportunities lie within you. You have the power to create, inspire, and achieve more than you ever thought possible. So go out there. Take the lessons you've learned, the goals you've set, and the dreams you've nurtured—and turn them into reality.

This isn't the end of your journey—it's the beginning. The best is yet to come.

My Journey

Success often looks effortless from the outside. People see the accomplishments, the accolades, and the life you've built, and they assume it all came easily. But for me, the journey to where I am today was anything but simple. It was a path marked by determination, self-discovery, and an unshakable belief in my ability to create something extraordinary.

I'm Randi Lynn Quigley—wife, mother, realtor, coach, and someone who knows what it means to build a life of purpose and passion. My story isn't just about real estate; it's about finding the courage to embrace challenges, learn from experiences, and create a fulfilling life rooted in faith, family, and resilience.

A Humble Beginning

I didn't grow up surrounded by luxury or privilege. My childhood was spent in a modest three-bedroom condo, shared with my mom and two sisters. My parents divorced when I was young, and my father lived about 45 minutes away. While I saw him every other weekend and on Wednesday nights for dinner, much of my upbringing was shaped by my mom's unwavering work ethic and determination to make ends meet.

From a young age, I learned the value of self-reliance. My siblings and I were expected to contribute, solve problems, and take care of ourselves in many ways. Those lessons stuck with me, shaping the way I approached challenges and opportunities later in life.

Discovering My Drive

After college, I followed what felt like a safe and predictable path into accounting. I was good at it, but something was missing. I craved connection, creativity, and a career that aligned with my passions. I didn't know it then, but real estate would eventually become that outlet.

My first foray into real estate wasn't glamorous. I didn't have a network of wealthy clients or a stack of leads waiting for me. What I did have was grit, a willingness to learn, and a deep desire to help people. Little by little, I built my business, focusing on relationships, trust, and an unwavering commitment to excellence.

From Realtor to Influencer

As my real estate career grew, I realized I had a unique ability to connect with people—not just in person, but online. I began sharing my story, my insights, and my day-to-day life on social media, building an audience that valued authenticity over perfection.

Through Instagram, Facebook, and other platforms, I started showing the real side of real estate: the challenges, the triumphs, and the human connections that make this work so meaningful. Whether it was a behind-the-scenes look at a home staging, a candid post about balancing work and family, or a tip for first-time buyers, my content resonated with people who were looking for more than just another realtor—they were looking for someone they could trust.

That online presence became a key part of my brand. It wasn't just about marketing homes—it was about building relationships, inspiring others, and creating a community.

Building a Legacy

Today, I'm proud to say I've achieved things I once thought were impossible. From producing millions in annual sales to being featured on national television as a host for The American Dream, my career has taken me to places I never imagined. But the most rewarding part of this journey isn't the numbers or the recognition —it's the impact I've been able to make.

I've helped families find their forever homes, guided sellers through emotional transitions, and mentored new agents who are now thriving in their own careers. Each of these experiences has reminded me why I chose this path in the first place: to make a difference.

A Life Rooted in Faith and Family

While real estate is a huge part of my life, it's not the only part. My family is my foundation. I'm now happily remarried, living on a beautiful farm with my husband, who's a farmer, and our four amazing children. Our days are filled with the simple joys of life— hiking, fishing, horseback riding, and enjoying the peace that comes with being surrounded by nature.

My faith has also been a guiding force in everything I do. It's what keeps me grounded during the busy seasons, gives me strength during the challenging ones, and reminds me to approach every day with gratitude. I strive to live a God-centered life, and I'm proud to be part of a community that shares those values.

Stepping into Coaching

One of the most exciting chapters of my journey has been stepping into a coaching role. Partnering with Grant Cardone and embracing the 10X philosophy has allowed me to expand my impact far beyond real estate. Coaching has given me the opportunity to mentor other professionals, help them unlock their potential, and create ripple effects of success in their own lives.

For me, coaching isn't just about teaching strategies—it's about empowering others to dream bigger, take massive action, and build lives they're proud of. It's about showing them that no matter where they start, they have the power to create something extraordinary.

Lessons I've Learned Along the Way

If there's one thing my journey has taught me, it's that success isn't about luck or circumstances—it's about mindset, resilience, and the willingness to do the work. Here are a few lessons I carry with me every day:

1. **You're Stronger Than You Think:** Life will throw challenges your way, but you have the strength to overcome them. Trust yourself and keep moving forward.
2. **Authenticity Wins Every Time:** People are drawn to real, relatable stories. Don't be afraid to show who you truly are—it's your greatest asset.
3. **Never Stop Learning:** Whether it's through books, mentors, or experiences, commit to growth. The more you invest in yourself, the more you'll be able to give to others.
4. **Success Is About Service:** At the end of the day, it's not about how much you achieve—it's about how many lives you touch. Focus on creating value, and success will follow.

What's Next

As I look to the future, my goal is simple: to keep growing, keep learning, and keep inspiring others to do the same. Whether it's through real estate, coaching, or simply sharing my story, I want to show people that anything is possible with the right mindset and a willingness to take action.

This isn't the end of my journey—it's just the beginning. And I'm so grateful to have the opportunity to share it with you.

A Note to the Reader

As you close this page of the book, I want you to pause and reflect—not just on what you've read, but on what it means for your own journey. If nothing else, remember this: *your potential is greater than you can imagine.*

Every step I've taken, every risk I've embraced, and every lesson I've learned has brought me to this point. And if there's one thing I've come to understand, it's that the only limits we truly face are the ones we set for ourselves.

So dream big. Bigger than feels safe. Bigger than feels possible. Build your bubble of potential—your space where ideas, ambition, and growth thrive. Fill it with positivity, resilience, and people who believe in you. Protect it fiercely and expand it endlessly.

This isn't the end of a chapter—it's the beginning of yours. Whether you're stepping into a coaching role, taking your real estate business to the next level, or pursuing a dream you've only dared to whisper, the path forward is yours to create.

The key is to start. Take one step, and then another, and then another. Action fuels momentum, and momentum leads to greatness. Even when the road feels uncertain, trust that every step forward is a step toward something extraordinary.

As you turn this page, take with you the belief that you are capable of more than you've ever imagined. The tools, the strategies, and the insights are here—but the spark to ignite your journey lies within you.

Now, it's your time. Dream boldly, act fearlessly, and create a life that reflects the limitless potential that's already inside you. I can't wait to hear your story of success.

Here's to turning this page into the first step of your greatest chapter yet.

With unwavering belief in you,

With gratitude,

- Randi Lynn Quigley

www.ingramcontent.com/pod-product-compliance
Lightning Source LLC
Chambersburg PA
CBHW071551220526
45469CB00003B/980